Honouring resistance and building solidarity: Feminism and narrative practice

by Loretta Pederson

Dulwich Centre Publications
Adelaide, South Australia

ISBN: 978-0-6459558-2-6

Copyright © Loretta Pederson 2024

This book was produced on the land of the Kaurna people, and it describes work
in Country around Australia. Dulwich Centre Publications acknowledges the
Traditional Owners of Country and pays respect to Elders past and present.

Dulwich Centre Publications
Halifax St PO Box 7192
Kaurna Country, Adelaide, South Australia, 5000.
dulwich@dulwichcentre.com.au
www.dulwichcentre.com.au

Contents

Publisher's note:
Feminisms, intersectionality and narrative practice

This book is part of a wider "Feminisms, intersectionality and narrative practice" project at Dulwich Centre. This project is engaging with current developments in thinking and action in relation to gender diversity and intersectionality, and the challenges and opportunities these pose for the field of narrative practice. In the 1980s, feminist ideas transformed the family therapy world and were a key impetus in the development of what has become narrative therapy and community work. Now, 35 years on, it seems vital that intersectional feminist ideas are once again brought to the fore to shape the future directions of narrative practice.

In the first phase of this project, practitioners from a wide range of contexts made short videos about why intersectional feminism is relevant and important to them.

The next phase of the project involved the creation of a special position at Dulwich Centre: the Chair of Feminisms, Intersectionality and Narrative Practice. There are two current chairs: Tileah Drahm-Butler and Sekneh Hammoud.

Zan Maeder then played an influential role, along with Tileah, Sekneh and other members of the Dulwich Centre team, in creating a rigorous free online course entitled Feminisms, Intersectionality and Narrative Practice. This course can be found at: www.dulwichcentre.com.au/feminisms

A further development in this project has been a Fellowship recently awarded to Tiffany Sostar for their projects in support of trans lives. The first of these has been published in *International Journal of Narrative Therapy and Community Work* (Sostar, 2024)

Significantly, this project also involves the publication of a series of books:

- *Pathways beyond despair: Re-authoring lives of young people through narrative therapy* by Angel Yuen (2019)

- *Justice-doing at the intersections of power: Community work, therapy and supervision* by Vikki Reynolds (2019)

- *Intersecting stories: Narrative therapy reflections on gender, culture and justice*, featuring contributions by Tileah Drahm-Butler, Jill Faulkner, Alyssha Fooks, Sekneh Hammoud-Beckett, Renee Handsaker, Simangaliso Brenda Nyoni and Carla Galaz Souza (2020).

The book you are holding in your hands, *Honouring resistance and building solidarity: Feminism and narrative practice* by Loretta Pederson, is the latest in this series. We're delighted to be publishing this book, which weaves together narrative practices, feminist principles and stories of Loretta's therapy conversations. We hope it offers company and ideas for your practice.

Who knows what future directions this project will take, but let's continue the conversations!

Warmly,
Cheryl White

Sostar, T. (2024). Care for trans lives [Audio recording]. *International Journal of Narrative Therapy and Community Work*, (1), https://doi.org/10.4320/VYKP6507

Acknowledgments

Thank you to the women who have inspired me with their acts of resistance and reclaiming, and who generously allowed me to share their stories in this book. Thanks to Cheryl White and David Denborough for support and encouragement during the writing and editing process. Many thanks to Claire Nettle for editing and helping me articulate my thoughts more clearly, and to Claire and David D for challenging me to read more widely, making this a better book.

Thanks to Angel Yuen, Manja Visschedijk and Jill Faulkner who offered thoughtful and rigorous feedback. Your precious time, energy and contributions are much appreciated. Thanks again to Manja and also to Marnie Sather for our discussions about the ways the established systems are letting down our families and the communities we work with, the complexities of responding in the here and now, and the hopefulness of dreaming of a different future. Thanks to Frankie Hanman-Siegersma and Zan Maeder for your thoughts and insights about gender identity. Thanks to Tileah Drahm-Butler and Kylie Dowse for our conversations about racism, power and privilege in Australia. I appreciated your wisdom and questions very much. Thanks to Larissa Minniecon whose questions about Chapter 9 invited me to think more deeply about the intersections of race and class.

Thank you to the strong and wise women who as narrative practitioners themselves have supported my growth and confidence: Marilyn O'Neill, Gaye Stockell, Carolyn Markey, Sekneh Hammoud and the team at Hope Connect, who have been with me throughout my narrative practice journey.

Thanks to Sekneh for your continuous support and encouragement during supervision and beyond, as we grapple with the complexities of this work and of living life. Thanks also for your help with working cross-culturally and for your thoughtful suggestions regarding Chapter 4. I have fond memories of conversations with Cheryl White, Jane Hales and Kelsi Semeschuk about the histories of feminism and narrative practice. Thank you for these enriching and inspiring conversations. Thank you to David Newman and Fiona Dicker for believing in my abilities and for helping me navigate hard times.

Thank you so much to Michael, Georgia and Eidan Pederson for your love and encouragement. Also, thanks to Georgia for your help and insights in editing my early drafts. Thanks, Dad, for believing I could get this book finished! Thanks, Mum, for all you have done and all you continue to do. You continuously love, encourage and inspire me.

An earlier version of Chapter 5 was published in *International Journal of Narrative Therapy and Community Work* (2015, number 3). It is included here with permission.

Introduction

What fills me with joy is walking alongside people as they step outside of a situation and look at it from fresh angles. What is happening in their context and how is that contributing to the current situation? Who is around when the problem is bigger? When does the problem take up less space? What ideas or beliefs add to the problem? This curiosity shapes conversations that often bring to light the influence of racism, sexism, homophobia, class-based disadvantage and discrimination, and other forms of oppression. I also get to hear about the actions people are taking to respond to these forces. As we explore together the skills, knowledges and values that have supported them in good times and in hard times, new options for action seem to light up.

In this book, I share practice stories of supporting people who are responding to hard times and injustice. I also look at history and culture to develop new understandings and highlight previously neglected stories of resistance to oppression.

I am a white middle-class woman working in Sydney on the lands of the Burramattagal people of the Dharug Nation and on the lands of the Cammeraygal people of the Eora Nation. Generations ago, my family came from Ireland and England to this land, hoping to start a better life with new opportunities. They made their homes on Country that had been invaded and colonised by the British government. When the Australian Government was established, it continued the racist ideas and actions of domination of local people and of Country. State-sanctioned massacres over a period of 140 years killed approximately a million First Nations people in an attempted genocide (Sentance, 2022). The Australian Government also attempted to eradicate First Nations cultures and languages through the forced removal of children from their families and communities, known as the Stolen Generations. First Nations people resisted, fought back and are continuing to resist ongoing colonisation and state-based violence. Growing up with white privilege shaped my experience of life and my viewpoint. Acknowledging and addressing this is ongoing work. I also live with cisgender privilege and benefit from being in a heterosexual relationship. In this book, I explore ways that I seek to address power and privilege in my practice, and I invite other practitioners to examine this too.

This book shares stories of many people who have come into my life through my work in counselling, case management and group work. I most often work with cisgender women, and their experiences form the centre of this book. I meet less frequently with trans women and men, nonbinary and genderqueer people, and cisgender men, all of whom are affected in similar and different ways by patriarchy and oppression. Their stories have stayed with me, inspiring me and informing the work described in this book. It has been significant to me when people of all genders have shared some of the ways they respond to the effects of oppression, including acts of resistance, protest, care, protection for self and others, and acts of reclaiming life. The stories people have shared with me have ripple effects on others' lives as I seek opportunities for connection and collaboration. I hope that the stories I share in this book will inspire other practitioners to be on the lookout for small but potentially significant actions taken by people who are experiencing hard times and injustice. Readers who take this practice into their own contexts will create further ripples.

About this book

This book is a practical resource for new and experienced practitioners in a range of contexts, such as counselling, mental health support and community work. It contains examples of narrative questions, possible directions that might be travelled, stories of practice, transcripts and prompts for reflection. These are offered to spark your own thinking, not as instructions to be followed. You can choose which ideas you might use, which you might alter, and of course, you can create new questions and approaches that fit your local context and the particular conversation.

Narrative therapy is a feminist approach, and feminist principles are embedded in the narrative practices I describe. Throughout the book, I highlight these connections and invite readers to reflect on the values and principles underpinning their own work. Although many of the stories in this book arise from experiences of cisgender women, the feminism described in this book seeks to build solidarity and mutual support among cisgender women, trans women, nonbinary and gender-fluid folks and others seeking an end to patriarchy and domination.

Pseudonyms have been used for the people whose stories are shared. Most have chosen their own pseudonyms and have been active in collaborating on which parts of their stories are included here and how they're told. Where possible, they have read and revised the relevant sections of the book.

The first chapter introduces my passion for narrative practice and for feminism. The following chapters set out further links between narrative practice and feminism. Each chapter highlights stories of women who are responding to hard times and injustice, and seeking connection with others in the face of marginalisation and oppression.

Throughout the book, there are examples of how practitioners can bring current news events, music, films, podcasts and other resources into the counselling room to explore the social contexts of problems and offer resonance with other people's stories. This can create a sense of solidarity with others in similar circumstances, and spark a realisation that apparently individual experiences sit within broader social and political contexts. A significant context for many of the women who contributed their stories to the book has been the #MeToo movement. Recognising a connection with women who have publicly shared their stories, and then examining their own stories in the light of this movement, has brought a political perspective that has decreased any sense of shame and isolation.

The final chapter considers ways of engaging with spirituality as a potential source of sustenance in hard times. It explores ways we can respect a person's beliefs while also increasing their sense of agency in situations where their sense of self and sense of choice has been negatively affected by traumatic events. Some folks have told me they have felt uncertain about raising the topic of spirituality among their friendship group or in counselling and have been appreciative when we made space for these conversations.

My hope is that readers of this book will become more confident in exploring the social and political contexts of individualised problems. I also hope that readers will notice their curiosity and hopefulness expanding as they engage with these stories and with the opportunities for reflection at the end of each chapter.

1.
A personal connection to feminist narrative practice

When I first encountered narrative practice, I saw it as a set of questions and ideas that might be useful at work. I vividly recall it becoming much more than that when I read about a project documenting the experiences of children who, like me, had grown up with a parent with mental health difficulties (Russell, 2006). Through engaging with the questions posed in this project, I began to see narrative practice differently: it became a passion and a way of examining and understanding the world. The project invited practitioners to gather stories using a series of questions designed to elicit double-storied accounts. These questions prompted me to reconsider my mother's experiences of life and my own responses to the difficulties our family faced in relation to her mental health struggles.[1] I began to link my experiences to those of other children and young people, and this sense of resonance was very comforting. I was excited by the idea of documenting and making visible the skills and knowledge that children develop through responding to family difficulties.[2]

---

[1] I did not end up contributing to this project. The stories that emerged from these questions can be found in Kis-Sines et al. (2008).

[2] Michael White, the co-originator of narrative therapy, was very interested in ensuring that children's skills in caring for themselves and others were acknowledged and not reduced to the negatively connotated concept of "parentification".

As well as acknowledging difficulty and complexity, the project invitation acknowledged and honoured the acts of care and love that are offered by a parent even when they are struggling with mental health difficulties. These actions, thoughts and intentions may have previously been unnoticed or less visible.

I was later introduced to another article by Shona Russell (2001), and I was very moved by her consideration of how things might have been different for her mother had the *context* of her mental distress been considered by professionals. This work made me reflect on the societal factors that contributed to the troubles my mother had encountered. I noticed that over all these years, she had been working hard to respond to the effects of patriarchy and some oppressive elements of religion (and the connection between these). She also faced dominant understandings of mental illness as a child and young person in the 1950s and 60s, and dominant ideas about "mothering when experiencing mental illness" in the 1970s and 80s. I had always been aware of my mother's love and care for us, but at times, a sense of uncertainty and worry for her wellbeing took centre stage. In thinking this through, additional memories of her acts of care became visible to me, coming out from behind the uncertainty and worry that surrounded her mental health struggles. As David Newman expressed it, "Deliberately recalling these stories somehow made others light up in my mind" (as quoted in Russell, 2006, p. 64). These newly remembered stories raised my curiosity and got me asking Mum about how, despite what she was going through, she had engaged in these acts of care for me, my siblings and others (including foster children, elderly neighbours and community members experiencing suicidal thoughts). Hearing these stories and then thinking about the social and political context also had me asking for stories about her responses to difficulty and her acts of resistance to oppression. It was wonderful to hear about her overt and covert actions to respond to the misuse of power by others. Mum was very relieved when I asked about these things and when I acknowledged her care and her efforts. She said, "I've been so worried that you would only remember the hard times".

This has contributed significantly to my work as I have had conversations with many women who are parenting while experiencing what is called "mental illness". Many are under the gaze of child protection services, and this brings additional fear, pressure and anxiety. It is interesting that fewer men than women have spoken with me about mental health struggles, and when young people speak to me about their parents, often the stories are about their mother's parenting, or their mother's experience of depression or a bipolar diagnosis. The paper "Children, parents and mental health" (Kis-Sines et al., 2008) suggests important questions about why this might be – questions about discourses around women and also around men, which may make some stories more visible than others:

> Is this due to the fact that women still do the vast majority of caring for children in most cultures?

> Is it that women, even when debilitated by mental illness, try to do all they can to sustain a connection with their children?

> Are men less likely to want their stories shared? Are they more likely to keep their stories of mental health difficulties quiet, silent, private, and perhaps to expect the women and children in their lives to do similarly?

> Are children and women more likely to take steps to cover up the mental health issues of men, or to explain them differently, to call them something else? To locate them elsewhere? (Kis-Sines et al., 2008, p. 5)

These questions have shaped my work by inviting me to enquire about what makes it possible for people to speak about family members who have experienced mental health issues, and what makes it more difficult. These cultural considerations alert me when a father is not mentioned, reminding me to gently enquire about whether the person has a father, and if so, his role and past and current circumstances. These questions also have me wondering about little clues men or their family members offer, such as when they mention that "Dad is always really stressed out" or "Dad drinks a lot, especially when he's worried". Some men have told me that these descriptions of troubles are generally considered more acceptable for men than naming them as anxiety or depression. I am keen to help explore the efforts that parents make to maintain connection with their children despite troubles. I am curious about how women's stories are told and by whom.

I am curious about why women's experiences of distress or their responses to hard times and injustice are so often framed as mental illness.

My mother's stories remind me to remain vigilant about drawing attention to societal factors affecting the people I meet with, and to enquire about the effects of conversations that consider these societal factors. The feedback I have had is that these conversations bring new understandings and are liberating. This has spurred me on in collaborating with women to explore the history of what is known in their lives as "mental illness". What has become clear to me over years of working with women is the link between past or current abuse and significant mental distress, which becomes labelled and medicated. It has been significant to discuss the role patriarchy plays in the occurrence of abuse, and the societal ideas and institutions that encourage the silencing or disbelief of people who have been abused within their family, within their school or religious institution or within the psychiatric system. Linking ongoing distress and concerns like drug use to the effects of patriarchy has been powerful for the women I meet with. We then consider their acts of resistance, of protest, of care, of protection for self and others, of reclaiming life – this has been very significant for the women, and also for my own sense of being sustained in this work (this is further discussed in Chapter 5). In some of these conversations, I might use more familiar language to scaffold the concept, rather than using terms such as "patriarchy".

Another turning point for me was when I experienced a time of ongoing "personal" crisis. Being encouraged to look at this from a feminist perspective got me jumping into theory and seeking out conversations with strong women who were also narrative practitioners. The idea that "the personal is political" (Hanisch, 1969) and the "personal is the professional" (C. White & Hales, 1997) got me again examining societal factors that contribute to the troubles in our lives, and the ways we can use our hard times to contribute to the understandings we have of our work. I was encouraged to think about how my hard times could sharpen my practice. I became aware that my ways of listening to the people I was meeting with were changing: I was becoming even more curious. I also noticed that I was more focused on looking out for small acts of resistance to the problem, or small exceptions to the problem story, rather than looking for grander examples. Having a close connection to pain and struggle helped me really understand how significant it can be when people take seemingly small steps. I was drawn to this quote from bell hooks:

> I came to theory because I was hurting … I came to theory desperate, trying to comprehend – to grasp what was happening around and within me. Most importantly, I wanted to make the hurt go away. I saw in theory then a location for healing. (hooks, 1991, p. 1)

And I found there was a lot more in her writing that I connected with:

> When our lived experience of theorizing is fundamentally linked to processes of self-recovery, of collective liberation, no gap exists between theory and practice. Indeed, what such experience makes more evident is the bond between the two – that ultimately reciprocal practice wherein one enables the other. (hooks, 1991, p. 2)

Thinking about the strength of my mother during her experiences of hard times, and her determination to hold on to life, also had me appreciating my grandmother and the challenges she faced raising 10 children under financial pressure. I remember she drew much strength from her faith, and certain images of beauty and quiet faith stand out to me, such as Grandma lighting a candle to remind her to pray for our safety as we travelled home to Sydney after our visits. However, as I have grown older, I think also of the social and political pressure she may have experienced as a woman and a mother from the 1940s onwards within the constraints of a strict Catholic patriarchal marriage.

During the "personal" crisis I mentioned, I framed a photo of my grandmother and took it to my office, drawing on the idea of a "club of life" (M. White, 1997) and the importance of a support team. I looked to her for strength and encouragement. When I look at this photo now, I see the determination on her face, and I feel her love again. I imagine her saying, "I love you. You can keep going". I still remember her warmth, her great hugs and the way she rocked back on her heels when she laughed. These memories of my grandmother also connect me to my mother, who enjoys much fun and laughter, and who gives wonderful, nurturing hugs. I think about what this heritage of love, compassion and care from these two strong women has brought to my life, and how it filters down to my own daughters and to my work.

****

Through sharing and honouring the stories of my mother, my grandmother and my own experience of struggle, I hope readers will pause and consider the people and circumstances that have shaped their own ways of working.

The next chapter demonstrates the use of narrative practice to highlight acts of resistance to domestic violence[3] and acts of reclaiming lives from violence and drug use. The sharing of individual stories is extended through linking with others to build solidarity among women who were previously isolated. Violence is explored as a social and political issue, rather than as an individual experience, and I show how feminist understandings underpin the narrative practices used.

---

[3] Various terms are used worldwide. I have used the term "domestic violence" to refer to a pattern of abusive actions by an intimate partner or ex-partner, which may include emotional abuse, financial control, tactics of isolation, sexual violence, intimidation and physical violence.

Reflection

- What first drew you to narrative practice?

- Is there an article or presentation that has spoken deeply to you, or been integral to shaping your work? What specifically stood out to you? What effects has this had on your work or life?

- Who in your family, workplace or friendship network has inspired you? In what ways have they contributed to your work?

- How have you navigated your own hard times while being involved in this type of work?

- In what ways has your practice been sharpened through your experience?

2.

The mountainous journey:
Moving from individual to collective stories

As London[4] described all she had left behind in regional New South Wales, she burst into tears. "I had to leave him. I had to get away from the violence and all the put-downs, but I didn't want to leave my family and friends and take my kids away from their cousins. Now we are here in Sydney, and he doesn't know where we are. But we are stuck in this flat. The kids have had to start at a new school, and they keep asking me when they can see their cousins. They miss them so much. I don't have any friends, and I'm so lonely. Have I done the wrong thing?"

In this chapter I describe ways we can explore domestic violence as a social issue and move from an individual focus towards connecting to the experiences of others. The intention in this type of work is to support the person who is attending individual counselling to shift away from an idea that "there is something wrong with me" to an understanding that the problem is with the violence they have been subjected to and the attitudes and institutions in society that support the use of violence. Another intention is to highlight the ways people have responded to violence and to connect their stories and actions to the stories and actions of others. This can reduce a sense of isolation and open ways to develop solidarity. It provides a foundation for further action on a societal level.

---

[4] "London" chose this pseudonym to connect her to the women in her family who came before her, and their choice to start a new life in a new place as she too had done.

This chapter explores the use of a "rite of passage" metaphor (M. White, 1995a) when working with people who are making significant changes in their lives, such as moving location, leaving a violent relationship, or separating themselves from drug use and drug culture. The use of collective documentation and sharing documents between people in individual counselling is also demonstrated, beginning with London's story.

The journey away from violence

I felt so moved by London's dilemma. I had met with her a few times in her flat. Each time, London would cry and describe a feeling of being "torn". Rather than responding to the invitation to assess whether or not she had made the right decision in moving to Sydney, I invited London to revisit the reasons she had left the relationship with Peter, and how this connected with the hopes she had for herself and her kids. London explained that she had two main reasons for choosing to move to Sydney: 1. to get away from violence; 2. to get away from the drug culture that Peter and her family and friends were involved in. Prior to making this big decision, London had tried to get her partner, Peter, to stop using violence.[5] When that wasn't possible, she had tried to leave the relationship a few times. She had stayed with family, but they were close friends with her partner and assured her that "he's a good bloke" and said that she was "really upsetting him" by leaving. London wanted to stop using drugs but had been finding it difficult as her family were using and selling drugs. She described it as "really in my face all the time, which made it pretty hard to stop using".

At the time I met her, London had not used any drugs in several months. After moving to Sydney, London felt the only way to keep herself and her children safe from physical violence and intimidation by her ex-partner was to keep her location secret. She was concerned that if she met up with any of her family members, they would tell Peter where

---

[5] Those on the receiving end of domestic violence are often expected by society to take on responsibility for stopping their partner from using violence. Part of our work is to question this expectation and help make visible that the responsibility for ending violence sits with the person who is using it.

she was. I supported London to articulate her hopes, intentions and values of safety and a drug-free environment for her children to grow up in. But the loneliness kept swamping London. This had been labelled as "depression" by the local community health centre. The loneliness also brought the confusion, which had London questioning her decision. I felt I needed something more in my approach beyond externalising the problem, placing the problem in context, and exploring the skills and values connected to the steps London had already taken (M. White, 2007).

I started to think about the rite of passage metaphor, which I had heard Michael White describe at a workshop I attended in 2006 as an important part of his work with women who were leaving a relationship in which they had been subject to violence and control. This concept had also been used with people who were changing their relationship with alcohol or drugs (Hegarty et al., 2010; M. White, 2000a), so it seemed applicable to both aspects of why London had left her previous locality. In this therapeutic use of an anthropological metaphor (after Turner, 1969; van Gennep, 1909/1960), Michael White (1995a) used the idea of a rite of passage to describe a "migration of identity". This is a three-stage process involving separation, liminality and reincorporation. In practice, people move back and forth in their steps towards their preferred lives, so the journey is not always linear.

White described therapeutic examination of the "separation" stage as involving exploration of the ideas, knowledges, skills and values that contributed to the person's decision to leave a situation of violence. This exploration can be done before the person leaves. In London's situation, we looked back at this stage to help her stay connected to these ideas, knowledges, skills and values.

What particularly struck me about this metaphor related to the second stage, and White's description of the importance of acknowledging that during the liminal period, the person may experience some highs and lows, some sense of turbulence and confusion or even despair as they adjust to their new situation. For London, this new situation involved living in Sydney away from family, friends and the familiar school and sporting teams her kids were part of. Everything was new, and London was trying to start a new life without any established support network. Added to this were the financial burden of being a single parent without paid work, and the hours needed to transport her kids to sport, medical appointments and other places without a car. It made sense that London would be longing for her old community. White (personal communication, September 2006) said he noticed that this turbulent time often had women remembering the good times of the relationship and wondering if maybe the bad times had not been so bad. Exploring this as the middle phase of a three-stage process, and mapping this out, can suggest that despair is evidence of progress through the liminal phase, giving a sense of hope that this stage will eventually end, and that stage three, reincorporation, will begin (M. White, 1995a). In this third stage, the person feels more settled and has a sense of community, which supports the new preferred identity.[6]

In addition to this articulation and mapping of an individual's journey through the stages of migration, White would share the charts or maps with other women in a similar situation, helping them not only to predict and prepare for possible challenges, but also to feel a sense of solidarity with other women. This connection to others was missing in my work with London, and yet it connects with several feminist principles that underpin narrative practice and that I hold dear: that we make the social issue of violence visible, demonstrating that personal problems are often political problems (Hanisch, 1969); that we recognise that what is labelled "depression" is often "oppression" (Reynolds, 2013); and that we support a sense of solidarity and connection between people responding to hard times, rather than promoting the idea of an individualised, private effort towards addressing problems (Kitzinger & Perkins, 1993). Connected to these feminist positions is the principle within narrative practice that we support people to speak through us to others, knowing that their hard-won knowledge can be invaluable to others in difficult circumstances (Denborough, 2008).

London and I began exploring her rite of passage through a journey metaphor. I suggested various metaphors such as "crossing the river" (Hegarty et al., 2010), "going on a hike" and "climbing a mountain" to assist London to find her own metaphor. London came up with "hiking up a mountain", and we explored the first two stages with the following questions.

---

[6] An example of this process can be seen in White (1995a).

Preparing for the hike

- How did you know it was time to set out on your hike?
  Were there certain things that made it urgent to get started,
  or were you biding your time for the right weather?

- What did you do to get ready for the hike?

- Had you been on this sort of journey before?

- In what ways did these previous journeys prepare you?

- Were you expecting to be hiking up a mountain,
  or had you imagined a mild stroll through the bush?

- In what ways did you prepare your kids for the hike?

- What were your hopes and intentions in setting out
  on this hike with your kids?

The long days of hiking

- What challenges or obstacles have made the journey hard so far?

- How have you been responding to these challenges or obstacles?

- Have there been any downhill bits, or flat sections,
  or has it always been an uphill climb?

- Has anything made it easier?

- Who do you have with you on this hike as a support person
  or cheer squad? Is this person hiking with you, or are you carrying
  their voice in your thoughts?

- What do you have in your first-aid kit?

- What is nourishing you?

- What ideas, skills or qualities are your kids bringing with them
  to help the family keep going on this hike?

Underpinning this exploration was the work we were doing to make visible that the responsibility for the violence sat with her partner. This is a key principle of feminism, which guides narrative practice: examining the discourses that blame women, nonbinary folks and others for the violence they are subjected to, and for the effects of violence on children. It was Peter's ongoing use of violence that led to London having to move to Sydney. This knowledge was something to hold on to when London was experiencing the "overwhelming guilt" that had her feeling "like a bad mum" when she heard the children ask questions like "Why did you bring us to Sydney?" and "Why are you stopping us seeing our cousins and Dad?" or saying, "I miss my grandma!"

We also discussed the idea that Peter did not invent this system of abuse or coercive control himself. We explored some cultural teachings, ideas, norms and rewards that may have contributed to Peter feeling a sense of entitlement to control his partner and children and to use physical violence (Dowse, 2017; Hill, 2019; M. White, 2011). Throughout the discussions, we also kept noticing that London's story was part of a wider story of many women experiencing violence.[7] London agreed that we could chart her journey and eventually share this with other women. She liked the knowledge that she was part of a group of women who were taking steps to reclaim their lives from violence and its effects, even though we hadn't yet shared the story of her journey with others.

Over time, I noticed that London was getting really involved in her local community through volunteering at the school, making friends with other parents and helping out in the children's sporting clubs. We wondered together what her intentions were, and what the effects of these actions were on how she was experiencing "the hike". London said she had multiple intentions. One intention was to support the kids to make

---

[7] London and I were speaking about cisgender women in heterosexual relationships; however, it is important to note that rates of domestic violence in LGBTQIA+ relationships are similar to those of cisgender women in heterosexual relationships (Campo & Tayton, 2015; NSW Government, 2014). Because of intersecting forms of discrimination affecting the availability of and responses by services, additional barriers may exist for LGBTQIA+ people seeking help in relation to domestic violence (Campo & Tayton, 2015; Coumarelos et al., 2023).

new friends through sport. Another intention was for her to keep busy to leave less time for the loneliness and the confusion. Additionally, she had previously found that volunteering was a good way to make friends. She said that contributing was important to her and always had been. Tied to this was another intention: she was setting a good example to her kids of being community minded. Finally, London said she had witnessed some parents putting their kids down if their team didn't win, and that being involved in sport offered the opportunity to influence other parents to be supportive of their kids rather than being competitive in a negative way. The effects were that London was "feeling more settled", and that the kids were happy that they had friends who were coming over to play. We started to wonder if London was entering the final stage: reincorporation. London decided that reaching the top of the mountain would mark the end of her hike.

Getting to the top of the mountain

- How will you know when you have reached the top of the mountain?

- What will you be noticing?

- What might others be noticing?

- What is your guess about what the view will be like when you get there?

Towards the end of our work together, we did a review of the journey, and London realised that she had indeed reached the top. I was genuinely in awe of her skills and knowledges, and we discussed ways these might be shared with others. We used a pre-printed winding path drawing, and London plotted important points along the journey. I wrote down some quotes from our final conversation. I had written some of her words in my notes over the past year, so we were able to review these together to decide which parts of London's stories and wisdom to share with others in the future. She was pleased to be able to put her own words to her story – to have a sense of her voice being heard and that this voice could potentially reach other women. London named her story "The mountainous journey".

After finishing my work with London, I heard stories of economic disadvantage, domestic violence and subsequent drug use from many other women. What stood out to me was that they had all managed to pull their lives away from drug use *and* had left or were trying to escape violence but were finding it challenging on this new path. Like in the work with London, we explored the steps they had taken and the skills, knowledge and values that they drew on to prepare for this journey, to take the initial steps and to work towards building a new life. I again found the rite of passage metaphor (M. White, 1995a) very useful in these conversations, but now I could draw on London's story too.

Linking stories to foster solidarity

Inspired by an article by David Newman (2008) about documentation, I asked three women I was working with individually, Kaylie, Stacey and Jodie, if they would be interested in hearing from other women in similar situations to find out how they were getting through. My hope was to help them feel less alone, as it seemed strange that I was the only one who knew their stories of determination and love for their kids, alongside the difficult stories that were known to friends, and in some cases, to child protection services. London valued opportunities to contribute to others, so she was pleased to have her story woven into a collective document with the other women's stories. In the document we created, four women's experiences were linked and shared.

Applying an intersectional feminist lens (Crenshaw, 1991) to the combined stories, we could see that the women shared multiple areas of marginalisation and oppression, such as domestic violence, poverty and class-based discrimination, which converged to exacerbate their disadvantage. There were also differences in the oppressions experienced, as two of the women were also resisting racism.

There is a risk that counselling an individual person in a private setting can reinforce the idea that problems are individual in nature and worthy of shame and blame, and that the solution needs to be achieved by the individual (Denborough, 2008). This makes the social and political contexts of problems invisible and takes the responsibility and focus away from society-wide solutions and community-based initiatives. Hanisch (1969) and Kitzinger and Perkins (1993) critiqued psychology and therapy for these reasons. My process of documenting these women's stories wasn't social activism, but it was an opportunity for the women to notice and discuss with me that they had all been subjected to violence in intimate relationships, and that drug use was not only a *response* to the abuse, but that it had also been keeping them tied to these relationships because their partners were supplying them with drugs, or they were selling drugs together. The women had also been subjected to abuse or neglect as children and they were comfortable for me to share this information with each other. This created space to consider and discuss the use of power by men in their lives, and the use of power by the state. In this sense, the work was political because it opened opportunities to discuss power relations happening in the home and the links with power relations in society. As discussed by Faulkner (2020), women who have experienced child abuse and domestic violence or sexual assault often turn to alcohol or drugs to manage the distress. This can lead to involvement with police and potentially prison time. Naming drug use as connected to men's abuse of power can open up new areas of conversation and new understandings (Faulkner, 2020).

For three of these four women, the violence and drug use had resulted in the state child protection service becoming involved in monitoring their parenting – an example of domestic violence leading to being subjected to further systems of power. One of the women, Kaylie, was facing a possible prison term for selling drugs. Jodie, who is Aboriginal, had experienced racism, often being stopped and questioned by police, or suspected of shoplifting by shopkeepers. In our conversations, Jodie noted that she was also judged and stigmatised due to ideas about class and education. Jodie mentioned that she lived in an area of Sydney that was stigmatised by residents of other areas. A couple of the women spoke about the challenges of public housing, and how they had applied for a transfer from their previous residence to escape drug connections but had ended up being transferred to another place where drugs were easy to acquire. Poverty meant they could not choose a private rental in another area.

Jodie particularly valued the conversations about racism, class, sexism and poverty. She valued sharing her knowledge with me and hoped that this would help me understand her struggles and contribute to helping other women in her situation. Creating space where racism and other effects of colonisation, such as intergenerational trauma and loss of land and language could be discussed, acknowledging my learnings and striving to take these forward in my work, were some other ways I showed respect to Jodie and her stories and aimed to reduce my power as a privileged person and a practitioner. Despite such efforts, power differentials remain, and we must take care to investigate the effects of our conversations and actions as practitioners, and ensure it's not up to those who consult us to educate us.

There is excellent work being done by First Nations practitioners who have developed innovative and culturally appropriate ways to engage with First Nations families (see for example V. Davis, 2017; Dulwich Centre Publications, 2020; Wingard, Johnson, & Drahm-Butler, 2015). I am drawn to the work of Janneen Wanganeen (2022), who has written about decolonising our practice when working with families who are impacted by the child protection system, which disproportionately removes First Nations children from their families.[8] In addition to making such injustices visible in our conversations and trying to address power within therapeutic relationships, it is important to invite stories of resistance to these injustices and to elicit stories of community-based acts of care and protection. We can also draw attention to examples like the significant advocacy work being done by Aboriginal Elders in Grandmothers Against Removals to improve child protection workers' cultural understanding and increase the involvement of local Aboriginal communities in decision-making to prevent First Nations children being taken from their families and communities (see for example Grandmothers Against Removals, 2015).

---

[8] The "child protection" system resulted in more Aboriginal and Torres Strait Islander children being removed from their families and communities in the early 2000s than at any time in the preceding century (Gibson, 2013). In 2022, 42.8% of the children from birth to 17 years in out-of-home care were Aboriginal or Torres Strait Islander (Productivity Commission, 2024). In the general Australian population, only 6% of children are Aboriginal or Torres Strait Islander. Children who have been in out-of-home care are at increased risk of entering the juvenile incarceration system and experiencing other adversities such as health problems and homelessness (Australian Institute of Health and Welfare [AIHW], 2023). The number of Aboriginal and Torres Strait Islander children in juvenile detention is increasing (AIHW, 2022).

By speaking through me to each other (Denborough, 2018), the four women I was working with were able to consider the social issues they were all facing and their responses to these issues. Guided by the principle of double-story development, I documented their words about how and why they had left drug use and violent relationships behind. I also recorded their values, hopes, skills and wisdom. To represent this sense of a collective voice as well as their individual voices, I used a mixture of "we" and "one of us" and "some of us" in the document and used direct quotes from the women. We discussed how their stories resonated with the stories of many women they knew who had also suffered abuse and who had been drawn into drug use, and how they connected with other stories I had heard too, so we decided to include phrases such as "many of us".[9] As London and I had finished our work together, I made contact again to share the completed document with her, and to let her know the effects for the other women of hearing her story and contributing their own.

I have noticed that people who find it hard to appreciate and acknowledge their own skills and initiatives may be more able to appreciate and acknowledge the skills and initiatives of others. I hoped that through seeing their words in print alongside the words of other women, they might see their own actions in a new way and feel proud of the steps they had taken to forge a new life for themselves and their children.

The three women I was meeting with were all keen to share their stories and for me to compile them as a collective document, which I have included below, as long as they didn't have to meet face to face. Shame was still present. This was in part due to the responses of child protection services, which were focused on a deficit approach at that time and viewed staying in a relationship of violence or returning to it as "the woman's failure to demonstrate protective behaviour towards their children" (Dowse, 2017, p. 2). I have since noticed a change in New South Wales services, which have begun attending to "protective factors" and the efforts women make to respond to the violence and keep themselves and their children as safe as they can. There has also been a change towards attributing the responsibility for

---

[9] For further discussion on creating a collective document, and suggestions about how to gather material, collate themes, create an opening paragraph, and include a sense of the individual voice and the collective voice, see Denborough (2008, Chapter 2).

violence to the person who has used violence, rather than to those subjected to the violence. For the women who contributed to the document, the person who had used violence was their male partner (now ex-partner). For some of the women, shame was also connected to responses from others in the community who would not let their history of drug use go.[10]

To create the first part of the document, I asked questions about the separation stage: the skills, values and knowledges that had them deciding to leave drug use and the violent relationship, and the preparation needed to take the first steps.

Moving away from drugs and violence

Wanting a better life for our kids

In deciding to move away from drugs and violence, we all thought about wanting a better life for our kids. Many of us had very difficult times growing up, and we hope things will be different for our kids.

One of us said, "To decide that I wanted to live a life without drugs, I first had to realise that drugs were getting in the way of me making the life I wanted for my kids. I always wanted them to have a better life than I had growing up, but I could see that things were heading the same way".

Another of us said, "In deciding to move away from drugs, I thought about my kids. I wanted them to know different people – people who don't use or sell drugs. I wanted to protect them from knowing about the drug environment".

---

[10] Since this work took place, two papers have been published that creatively consider ways to externalise shame. Practitioners may find these useful in relation to group work. Kerry Major spoke with Aunty Barbara Wingard about the effects of colonisation on Aboriginal folks (in Wingard, 2015). Major came up with the idea using a "shame mat" for women to wipe their feet on when arriving to wipe away shame. Kylie Dowse (2017) described working to reposition shame with a group of men who had used violence. This allowed the men to find ways to describe how they had acted towards their partners and children without minimising their actions or their responsibility for the violence. I have written about working to externalise shame and trace the patriarchal history of shame during individual counselling in Chapter 6.

Some of us have experienced devastating outcomes of drug use. "I got to the point of hating drugs. Drugs took my child away – he was put in foster care by the child protection service. This was traumatic for me and my child and my extended family."

You have to be ready

"I so badly wanted to get off drugs, but I still had cravings. You have to be ready to stop using – you can't have 'one more'. This takes determination."

Kids notice more than you think

We have a shared hope that our children won't experience addiction.

"I know that kids are smart, and they notice more than you think. I don't want our kids growing up thinking that using drugs is an okay way to live. We have to teach them the right way."

"Kids have earlier memories than we might realise. I want to set a good example."

One person expressed this idea: "I want my kids to know about my experiences so that they will know that drugs aren't the right path. They will make their own mistakes, but I want to explain about my mistakes in a way that isn't hypocritical. I need them to know that addiction brings hardship".

Another said, "I wanted my kids to have a better life – a life without seeing violence. I don't want them to think that violence is standard in a relationship. I would hate for my daughter to be in a violent relationship, or for my sons to hit their girlfriends. I want to instil different morals. I want them to have respect for women and to understand women. I want them to know that women aren't there to be used for sex".

Moving out of the area

Some of us had to move out of the area where we had lived. These are our stories.

"I had to physically move away from my family and friends and not tell them where I was living because of the drugs and because they were friends with my ex. This was really hard because I had to start again and make new friends. The kids had to change schools. I was very lonely for a while and felt especially sad that my kids couldn't see their cousins. It seemed like the only way though, because everyone I knew at the old place was offering me drugs, and I thought hiding my whereabouts was safer for my kids and me because of the violence and put-downs from my ex."

"Once I decided to get off drugs, I realised I would have to leave town because everyone knew that I'd been selling drugs, and I couldn't walk down the street without being stopped several times by people wanting to buy. I also had to get away from a violent relationship. I had to leave my life, my family, and I couldn't get to my access visits with my kids who are in foster care. I miss them every day, but it seemed like the only way – I had to do it."

Kids have to be number one
"I watched the effects drugs were having on my friends and on their kids. I didn't like seeing them miss out on food. Kids have to be number one. I decided I didn't want to sell drugs anymore. I didn't want to be part of the reason that kids were missing out. I couldn't be part of that."

Knowing my son's hopes for me
"My son said to me, 'I don't want you selling drugs, Mum, and I don't want you getting hurt by bikers'. That helped me to stay focused on getting off drugs."

Having support
"I stayed with someone who helped me go cold turkey. She drove me to work and helped me put that money aside so that I could leave town. It meant a lot to me to have that support."

The second part of the document was about the liminal stage: the steps the women had taken, and the ups and downs they had experienced since commencing the journey. The women reflected on ways they were starting to feel more secure in their new life, even though not all identified as having reached the final "reincorporation" stage.

Getting through the hard times

You need determination to stay off drugs

"If you want to get off drugs and you want it that bad, you can do it. You have to make yourself do it – you can't expect other people to do it for you! You need determination not just to get off drugs, but to stay off."

I know my value

"I knew there was a better life because I'd had it before. My kids aren't living with me now, but when I see them, I want to be the kind of mother that they remembered – the one I was before drugs. I know my value. I want my kids to know my value."

"I knew that the way my boyfriend was treating me was not right. That stops me from going back to him. No-one deserves violence."

We help each other

We have all noticed the importance of friends who don't use drugs and who don't condone violence.

One of us said, "Eventually I was able to make different friends who don't use drugs. I did this by getting really involved in my kids' school and their sporting clubs. I've noticed that my new friends have different values and theories about life than my old friends, and they support me".

"Adults need moral support too – someone to lift you up when you're down. Having a supportive new partner who doesn't use drugs and having friends with similar values helps me to stick to my new life in the hard times."

Another of us said, "When stress might push me back to the bong, I go and visit my friend. We take the kids to the playground, and I like seeing our kids playing happily together. It helps by keeping me distracted and also having someone to talk to about the stress. She is trying to stay away from drugs too, so we help each other".

I remind myself that it's not worth going back on to drugs

"When I'm feeling down and get tempted, I remind myself that it's not worth going back on to drugs. I would lose the kids to the child protection service. A few hours of being numb is not worth that! If I lost the kids, my problems would be bigger, and the pain would be bigger, and the kids would be traumatised."

I write down my thoughts and feelings

"When I'm really upset, I write down my thoughts and feelings. This helps me assess how I'm feeling. It also gets the anger out on paper, so that I can calm down and speak to the person later without saying or doing something that might jeopardise the relationship."

"My kids aren't living with me right now, so I write down all the things I wish I could say to them. Also, when my counsellor is away on holidays, I write her a letter since we can't meet in person. When I am angry with someone, I write them a letter with all the things that can't be said. This helps me think things through so I can be more assertive and figure out how to handle the situation. I don't post these letters. Just writing them serves the purpose."

Try to let it go

"I've noticed that holding on to hate destroys me, so I try to let it go and forgive the person. This is hard, but it is better than letting it destroy me. I pray for the person in the hope that they might change."

"I've had to let go of hate, as I've realised that hate eats you up."

"For me, forgiveness isn't saying that what he did was okay. It is saying that what he did was wrong, but I'm going to choose to not hate him."

Focus on the good things
"Rather than focus on the difficult things or what I don't have, I focus on the good things that I do have."

Remembering my priorities
"When I'm down and worrying about money, I remind myself what is important. It is better to stand on my own two feet than to get into debt, or go back to the relationship, just to impress people with new things. Money isn't everything."

Seeing the strength of my kids
"My kids have been through hard things. Seeing their strength gives me hope that I can get through this."

My daughter knows how much I care about her
"Thinking about the love and trust my daughter has for me and the strength of our relationship helps me in the times when we can't be together. This also helps when people make negative comments about me or my parenting. I know that my daughter knows how much I care about her."

Making mistakes
"Getting through the hard times can be trial and error. You can either go one way or the other – it's your choice. Making mistakes has allowed me to learn how to deal with situations the right way."

Hold on to hope
"I call this journey 'The mountainous journey', as there have been ups and downs, and it hasn't been easy. I would encourage other parents trying to move away from drugs not to give up, and to hold on to hope. It can be hard, but you will get there!"

Throughout the process of creating this collective document, I shared the unfolding stories among the women so they could find their language through the language of others bringing to mind their own skills, hopes, values and intentions (see Newman, 2016). After drafting the document, I took it to each woman individually to ask for feedback and ensure she felt a sense of ownership. This was in line with the Charter of Storytelling Rights (Denborough, 2014). The women were so pleased to see their words reflected back to them, and all spoke of a sense of unity or connection with the other women, even though they had never met. This "invention of unity in diversity" (Freire, 1994, p. 157) and creation of "communitas" (Denborough, 2008, p. 41; Turner, 1969, 1979), in which there is a sense of shared unity among people who are going through a similar experience, is one of the hopes of collective narrative practice. This hope guided my process in collecting the stories and in including the themes and quotes in the document. It also connects with my experience of being supported by and supporting other women when we speak about our struggles and our responses to these struggles and make sense of these together. While acknowledging differences in our experiences and levels of privilege, such conversations can create an experience of solidarity (Hanisch, 1969; hooks, 1986). I have felt stronger for this feminist mutual support.

The four women were excited by the idea that, through me, they could share the document with other women I meet with in the future, and with other practitioners. Kaylie, who was facing the possibility of a prison sentence, had been contemplating studying a course in prison, so that after her release she could get a job supporting others with a problematic relationship with drugs or alcohol. She said, "I want to help other people. This [co-creating and sharing the document] is a start in using my experiences to help others".

Furthering connections through outsider witnessing

Around this same time, I was meeting with Debbie, who had stayed away from drugs for seven years. She had spoken with me about a sense of being "snubbed" by other parents at the local primary school. As we explored this further, she described it as "judgement and exclusion". Here are some questions I asked Debbie about this sense of judgement and exclusion:

- You mentioned being excluded by other mums, and you think this is because they assume you are using drugs. What are they doing that contributes to that sense of exclusion?

- What has given them this impression, when we both know it's been years since you've used drugs?

- You think it is because they know the suburb where you live, and also that they make assumptions about your values because you have several kids. What impact do these assumptions and ways of excluding you have on the way you see yourself?

- How does this affect your interactions and involvement at the school?

- Does this judgement and exclusion from people who aren't using drugs impact your determination to stay away from your old friends who are still using?

Debbie's comment about the suburb she lived in had us discussing class stigma. Debbie told me that her husband had been excluded by the other parents when he took their son to soccer training. He told Debbie he thought it was because the way he dressed marked him as not being middle class like the other parents.

Thinking about Debbie's own challenges with stigma, and the fact that she was further down the road of not using drugs than the women who had contributed to the collective document, I wondered if she might like to be an outsider witness (M. White, 2007) to the document. I thought some of the themes might resonate for her, and I guessed that she might be interested in contributing to a sense of solidarity for other women who were trying to stay off drugs. She readily agreed. I video recorded her response and then typed it into a letter for the authors of the document. Debbie did not want her face to be shown to the other women because they lived in a small community, and she didn't want to be recognised at the shops or at our groups.

These are the questions I used to assist Debbie to shape her response:[11]

- As you heard me read the document of the women's ideas
  and the steps they have taken, did any particular word or phrase
  or idea stand out to you?

- Why do you think that particular part stood out to you?
  Does it connect with your own actions or hopes or ideas?
  Is it similar or different to your experience?

- Having heard their words, do you have any guesses about
  what is important to the women?

- Thinking about these values, does a picture jump into your mind?
  It's okay if it doesn't, I just wondered if maybe an image popped in.

- What effect has hearing about this had on you?
  What are you thinking about?

- Keeping these thoughts in your mind over the next week or more,
  what effect might this have? Is there a step you might take?

I presented Debbie's responses, along with some responses from the women involved in creating the original document, as a letter. In the letter (and in this book) I used pseudonyms for all the women except for Stacey, who chose to use her own name as a political statement of pride in her achievements, and a stand against stigma. Here is the letter:

---

[11] These are based on Michael White's (2007) categories of enquiry for outsider witnesses.

Dear Kaylie, Jodie, Stacey and London,

I am writing to let you know about some of the effects of sharing your skills and wisdom in moving away from drugs and violence and getting through hard times.

In reading each other's words, some similar ideas emerged:

Jodie said, "It makes me happy for the other people. They have found a similar way to get through. To know they are fighting just as hard as me for a better life inspires me to keep going in the struggle".

Kaylie said, "It brings me hope to read other people's experiences and hopes – to know that there are other parents out there staying away from drugs".

Stacey said, "Remembering where I was keeps me going in staying away from drugs and alcohol. I feel good that my ideas are helping other people".

This was similar to Kaylie's hopes for sharing the document: "I want to help other people. This is a start in using my experiences to help others".

I invited another woman I know, Debbie, to hear your words and tell me her reflections. She and her husband have been off drugs for seven years. After I read Debbie the document, she said that she thought your words would be relevant for people trying to leave drug use behind and would also be relevant for people when alcohol use or gambling was affecting themselves and their families.

Debbie commented that it would be great to also hear from some dads who are leaving drug use behind. This may happen in the future through my own work or through sharing the document with other counsellors. Kaylie's response to the possibility of men reading it was: "That would be great! As mums we want dads to be off drugs too. We want our kids away from the drug environment. If our words can help men, that would be good."

Debbie felt connected to you in hearing your words, "I remind myself that it's not worth going back on to drugs". She said she tells herself, "Every day that we don't smoke pot is one more day we keep the kids". She told me, "We must remember what the hardships were that brought us to this point of a new life". She could also relate to the difficulty of choosing to distance yourself from family and friends who are in the drug culture, but Debbie felt that this is a very important strategy. If she sees her family, she chooses the time, place and activity to minimise the chance that drugs will be present.

Hearing about the efforts you are making for your kids, Debbie had the image of kids playing – happy and safe. She liked the strategy of taking the kids to the playground when stress is around.

Hearing your ideas, and the way you've each put in so much effort to move away from drug use and find new friends and new ways of getting through hard times, Debbie noticed that you each put thought into your decisions and have used a lot of determination. She described you as "smart". She said that drugs can rob people of their energy and motivation, and make it hard to use your potential, so she was really pleased that you are moving towards your hopes for your lives. She thought you must have used strength, knowledge and resources to do this. She had an image of cornfields and sunflowers, of growth and life. She called you "trailblazers" finding a new path for yourselves and your kids.

The idea of building support networks to get through hard times really resonated with Debbie. She wanted to acknowledge the possibility of relapse, and that it can take several attempts to finally get free from drug use. She wouldn't want shame to stop anyone "getting back on the horse". She emphasised the importance of friends and services, and that it is okay to ask for help. She said, "Find those resources that helped you the previous time".

Debbie found your words personally encouraging. She said, "It makes me feel less alone, less of an outsider. Sometimes my family make me feel like a black sheep for being drug-free and sober. It's good to know there are other like-minded people out there". It also reminded her of her hope to use her experiences to help others. She said the document made her more determined to do this.

Thanks for letting me share your skills and wisdom in this way. It has been a privilege to see the encouragement and support you have been able to offer each other. With the document now going on to our webpage and to other counsellors, I'm sure your words will have further ripple effects.

Warmest wishes,
Loretta

The women were very proud when I was invited to share their stories at the International Narrative Therapy and Community Work Conference in 2012. The idea that their knowledge could help sustain women all around the world, and support and educate practitioners, made them feel that their suffering "wasn't all for nothing", and that they were indeed contributing to the lives of other women who have faced injustice and abuse. Sharing their stories with pride was one small step the women took to address the hiddenness of domestic violence and the shame of drug use and child protection intervention.

Reflecting on the journey

In an effort to uphold narrative practice values in relation to the politics of representation (C. White & Kamsler, 2016), the person being the owner of their own story, and the feminist intention of raising women's voices, I have contacted as many of the contributors to the document and letter as possible to get their thoughts on them being shared again in this book. I was recently able to catch up with London. Our work together finished more than a decade ago, and her children have grown up. In discussing her journey, leaving her community and starting again in Sydney, I asked London about her reflections on the decision and the years of ongoing commitment that this took. London said, "It was the best decision – making a distance between myself and my ex and his violence, and between myself and my family while they were still using drugs. My kids are all grown up now and doing well. They have all finished school. None has a criminal record. They have jobs. Their lives have turned out much better than if they'd grown up around drugs".

I then asked London what acknowledging this does to that old voice of guilt. "I know I've done the right thing. I don't have to feel guilty for putting my kids first. I've got back in contact with my mum and my sister, who is now off drugs. My sister is doing so well and looks fantastic and healthy now. I love having her back in my life, and my kids love it too. She recently told me that I made the right decision, even though she resented me at the time." I asked London what this acknowledgment was like for her. She responded, "Good. It was great to hear that she is acknowledging what I went through and why I had to make that tough decision all those years ago".

We wondered what London might say to her younger self, the one who had grappled with the loneliness, the confusion and guilt. "I would tell myself, 'You are doing the right thing! It will be okay'." London said she was so pleased that she had been able to share her story to encourage other women, including through my conversations with other women, contributing to the collective document, and now printing her story in this book. She offers this encouragement to any women currently on the journey: "Keep going! You are on the right path, and you will get there."

****

This chapter has demonstrated the feminist principle of seeing the social and political aspects of problems that people are encountering in their lives by focusing on domestic violence and drug use, and touching on issues of state intervention and scrutiny, classism, financial disadvantage and stigma. Narrative practices described in this chapter included the rite of passage metaphor, collective documentation and enabling people to share stories with others through us as practitioners. The idea of strengthening people's opportunities to voice their experiences and concerns in their own words and finding ways to build solidarity between people facing similar social issues was introduced. In the next chapter, these ideas of voice and solidarity will be extended through discussion of work with people experiencing the effects of heteronormativity, homophobia and racism.

Reflection

- In your own communities, what ideas exist about people who use drugs?

- What names are given to people who use drugs?

- How would you characterise these ideas and attitudes?

- Are these attitudes amplified when the person who is using, or has used, drugs is a mother?

- Are the same ideas and attitudes present towards fathers? Why or why not?

- What are your own views about people who use drugs?

- What issues are prevalent in your community?

- Are you currently working on these issues as individual problems or as social and political problems?

- In reading this story of connection and solidarity, highlighting steps people have taken to move their lives in the direction of their hopes and values, what are you thinking about? What steps might you take in your own context?

3.
Voice and solidarity

The previous chapter shared examples of moving from a focus on problems as individual experiences to a focus on problems as reflecting collective concerns: that people's experiences reflect and embody social issues. As practitioners, we can invite people to speak not just to us, but "through us" to others with whom they have things in common (Denborough, 2008, p. 16). We need to actively work towards fostering connections among people so that counselling doesn't perpetuate notions of problems being individual in nature and in solution. This could include connections with other people we meet with, connections within the person's own networks, or as will be explored in Chapter 6, connections with public figures or social movements. In this chapter, I develop this theme of connections among people and stories by sharing ways of supporting people to voice their experiences, describe problems in ways that bring into focus the social and political contexts of their experience, and join with others. I call this "voice and solidarity". These stories were developed in individual and couples counselling in private practice.

Politicising anxiety, depression and self-hate and moving towards solidarity: Rose's story

Rose, who was in her early 20s, was meeting with me to reduce the effects of anxiety and depression on her life. Anxiety had come and gone at different times in Rose's life and had risen again recently. Depression had grown quite large in the past year and forced Rose to leave some work she valued in preserving threatened environments. In response to externalising questions, Rose described depression as a "grey thing" that flattened her emotions and left her feeling numb. When I asked, Rose could describe many things that contributed to this grey thing. One of these was damage to the environment caused by capitalist endeavours. She had many skills in managing this grey thing, and we explored the social history of these skills, who she learnt them from, and which values they were connected to. We also explored Rose's support team. During our conversations, I used the statement of position maps 1 and 2, re-authoring questions and re-membering questions (M. White, 2007). We both witnessed the ways Rose was taking back her life from the grip of anxiety and the grey thing.

As I asked more about who or what influenced her values, Rose shared with me her passion for feminism, queer theory and politics. Rose's strong heart for social justice was also very evident. This included justice for people and protection for the environment. We had some lively discussions about the effects of capitalism and patriarchy on society, particularly on women, and on the environment.

Rose described how self-hate had joined with anxiety and the grey thing to provide a commentary on her life – she called it an "insidious voice". I asked her what sorts of things the insidious voice of self-hate was saying, and she told me it was criticising her body shape. When exploring issues of body image, I find deconstruction questions helpful. Examining and questioning dominant discourses can shed light on the public and social nature and history of problems that people perceive to be private. Once these discourses are made visible, space becomes available for the person, family, team or community to choose whether to continue going along with expected thoughts and actions, or whether to choose another way of being and responding (M. White, 1992). Exploration can also occur about times when the person, family, team or community has already stood up to these sorts of expectations and demands. This process of asking questions to make discourses visible, and to examine their history, purpose and effects, is what I mean when I use the word "deconstruction".

I asked Rose where self-hate got its ammunition about her body shape: Who decides what is the right or good body shape? Is this idea universal or is it different in different cultures? Who benefits from cisgender women hating their body shape? Are people of other genders also affected by body shape discourses? After responding to some of the deconstruction questions, Rose concluded that "the insidious voice is a mirror of social messages". She wondered if perhaps the negative commentary of self-hate "is a microaggression against myself". I was quite taken by this response and appreciated how this thinking supported Rose to keep finding ways to step away from these socially constructed self-judgements. We both enjoyed feeling "fired up" against patriarchy during our conversations, and in thinking again about body image, Rose said, "capitalism needs us to hate ourselves". We then spoke about the fitness industry, the beauty industry, the media. Rose also raised some concerns she held about the connection between capitalism and the promotion of psychiatric medication, although she acknowledged that medication can be helpful. I continue to be inspired by Rose to stay close to my own efforts against the forces of patriarchy and capitalism.

The insidious voice was also attacking Rose's relationship with her girlfriend. Rose identified as lesbian and asexual. The self-hate commentary was accusing her of having an invalid relationship. Feminism and queer theory have long utilised deconstruction to question taken-for-granted ideas in society and to make visible the effects of patriarchy. Part of deconstruction is tracing the history of these taken-for-granted ideas, demonstrating that they had an origin – they don't just naturally and eternally exist. Narrative therapists Tilsen and Nyland (2010), drawing on Foucault (1978), have described the influence that the emerging field of psychiatry had during the 1800s on the categorisation of bodies and of sexual acts, and how this led to the categorisation of sexual identity. This categorisation had the oppressive intent to regulate norms (Tilsen & Nyland, 2010). Tilsen and Nyland (2010) explored how deconstruction is used by queer theorists such as Warner (1991, 1999) and Doty (1993) in their exploration of culture. When societal expectations are explicitly explored, this frees people up to make choices that fit with their values and hopes, rather than going along with the pressure to measure up (Tilsen & Nyland, 2010). Drawing on these queer theorists, I asked Rose some deconstruction questions:

- What ideas in society is self-hate utilising when it suggests your relationship is invalid?

- How long have these ideas been around in society?

- Where do you hear these ideas?
  Who benefits by reproducing or spreading these ideas?

At the time we were meeting, the Australian same-sex marriage debate was receiving much social media attention. The people of Australia were being asked to vote on whether or not the marriages of same-sex couples should be legally recognised. Many hurtful arguments were expressed about the validity and worth of same-sex couples' relationships and their children, and discussion spread to other issues such as gender identity. Misinformation circulated about school education on these topics, resulting in the defunding of a school-based anti-bullying program aimed at supporting teachers to address homophobia and cisnormativity in schools, which affects all young people, not just LGBTQIA+ young people. This was a painful time, and the pain is still being felt by the LGBTQIA+ communities[12] in Australia today. Rose questioned, "Why do other people get to vote on my life?" She saw the effects of this debate on her mental health, with anxiety and the voice of self-hate intruding on her life again after having been fairly quiet for some time. This reinforced for me the importance of asking questions about the contexts of people's lives. We also examined the skills and knowledges Rose had in limiting her exposure to these messages, and in finding avenues of support and connection. Some questions helped to bring forward rich and nuanced stories of support:

---

[12] At the time we were meeting, the acronym LGBTQIA+ was used to describe Rose's community. The term "sex, sexuality and gender diverse" was also commonly used to describe this community.

- Who understands your identity and supports you in this?

- Who makes you feel accepted?

- How do they do this?

- Who supports your relationship with your partner?

- What actions or words demonstrate this?

Rose's family and workplace were very supportive of her identifying as lesbian, but Rose had told me that people really struggled to understand asexuality, and at times cast doubt about her relationship with her girlfriend. We deconstructed many dominant ideas that Rose had heard about asexuality, such as:

- You must not have met the right person yet.

- This is just a phase.

- Perhaps you were abused and your sexuality is damaged.

- Counselling should "fix" you.

Therapy is not neutral in its effects. Asking questions is a political act: we can ask questions that open up exploration of ways to resist the status quo, or questions that shut exploration down. As well as making visible the influence of patriarchal and heteronormative messaging in society, narrative conversations can explore acts of resistance and of care or protection of the self or others. In the 1980s, Michael White and David Epston were bringing quite radical ideas to the field of family therapy, including

> the political idea (again inspired by both feminist and Foucauldian thought) that people can and do continually try to resist or refuse the formations of self proposed by the dominant culture, and that therapy can be a place to notice, elicit, and support people's acts of resistance and refusal. Indeed, this can be a very appropriate part of therapy

work. This is perhaps a radical re-conception of the understanding of therapy. (Ron Findlay, in C. White, 2016b, p. 22)

I asked questions to bring forward Rose's skills and acts of refusal, and to connect her responses to the responses of others in her community to build a stronger sense of support and solidarity:

- How have you managed to survive this difficult time of additional negative media attention?

- Were there skills you were drawing on from previous experiences of stigmatisation, microaggressions or bullying?

- Who supported you during this time?

- How are other people in your community responding to protect themselves or others?

- What does it mean to you when you see these actions of others?

- What would you call these actions you and others are taking?

Around this same time, I met with another woman of similar age who identified as lesbian and shared similar concerns about expectations about relationships. She was feeling very isolated, not knowing anyone else who was questioning these expectations. I asked Rose if I could share a bit of her story and her wisdom about responding to the negative comments she receives. Rose agreed. The other woman was surprised and pleased to hear about Rose's knowledge, and this inspired Rose and I to share her knowledge more widely. To do so, Rose created a document for other people I might meet with. She has generously allowed me to also share this with narrative therapy students, and with readers of this book. The document describes how challenging it can be to have a sexuality that is perceived as different and offers some tips for getting through this.

On being different: What I know about having a sexuality that people aren't familiar with

- Frequently, people will struggle to understand. They may compare it to something that is completely wrong or completely offensive. I think the thing that's worth remembering is that most of these comments aren't intended to make you feel awful. They might anyway, but once you get past that initial reaction, it can be worth persevering with the conversation, because if you can help them come to an understanding, then it's a win.

- The flip side of this is the feeling of being a walking example, and the thought that everyone deserves a window into your life. This isn't true. It's hard to know what information is worth sharing because it might help, and what is worth keeping to yourself because sharing it would be outside your comfort zone. Eventually, through trial and error, you start to figure out where the line is.

- Maintaining a sense of self-worth and validity is like playing a never-ending game of snakes and ladders. Setbacks might be a comment someone makes, a line in a novel, a song, a conversation, a look from a stranger. Your confidence in who you are and what you know about yourself suddenly takes a hit. Sometimes these setbacks feel like sliding all the way back to the beginning of the board, other times it's just a little dip, and occasionally something great happens and you get a boost. I guess the trick is to just keep playing.

- The thought that you're only worthy of love if you force yourself to change is dangerous.

- The thought that everybody in the world wants the exact same relationship model is completely false.

- You're going to need to remind yourself of those last two points constantly.

- People can and will surprise you in a good way. You can negotiate on your own terms to find happiness in a relationship, and there are people out there across the spectrum who will come to the bargaining table. There is no right way to love, and there is no one-size-fits-all relationship. And it's possible that a lot of people out there have been tricked into thinking they should have something that they don't even want. Maybe everyone else is walking around thinking that they're different, and thinking that it's something to hide and change. They might be relieved to meet you and hear your story and realise they're not alone.

- Whatever you are, there is a community for you out there. Thank God we live in the age of the internet and can find them so much more easily.

Written responses to Rose's document let us know that people have indeed been touched by what she shared. Some mentioned a sense of resonance with Rose's experiences and a liberation that came with hearing her ideas. Hearing these responses, Rose said she felt "warm – knowing someone is listening, someone hears you", and "honoured that they thought enough about what I said to write back".

In my work with Rose, I used feminist narrative practices of deconstruction and externalising to support her to voice her experiences of oppression and marginalisation. Speaking about the social and political contexts of the problems she was facing strengthened Rose's resolve to live life in her own way. I used re-authoring practices to explore and expand on Rose's skills and knowledges in responding to the microaggressions she was subjected to. We also explored her support networks in line with feminist narrative ideas of identity being socially constructed and of seeking support outside the therapy room. By speaking through me to another woman in a very similar situation, Rose felt a sense of solidarity, as did the other woman. In sharing her document, Rose received responses that some of her wisdoms resonated with people who may not identify as lesbian or asexual, but who nevertheless feel they don't fit heteronormative expectations of ways of being in relationship (see Warner, 1991).

Exploring the social and political contexts of people's lives in single-session work

In my previous volunteer work on a phone line for LGBTQIA+ folks, the conversations were one-off and anonymous, so I was not able to consult with people about whether they would be comfortable with sharing their stories here, or how they would like their stories to be represented. For this reason, I won't share detailed stories here. However, in listening to the problems and dilemmas people were facing, various themes emerged: exclusion from family or social networks, bullying at school or in the workplace, and the pain and distress these experiences caused. Like in my work with Rose, discussing the social and political contexts of people's experiences seemed to be useful. Trans people from regional towns or from families with strong religious beliefs, for example, seemed to be at particular risk of isolation, and spoke to me about fearing violence if they started wearing clothes that expressed their gender identity or acting in ways that didn't fit with society's expectations. We spoke about strategies they had used to survive. This sometimes included "flying under the radar" by trying to fit stereotypes about the gender they were assigned at birth. We also spoke about ways they were resisting these expectations. For some, these steps were named as "measured risks" or "small protests" and included ordering clothes online and wearing them alone in their bedroom, or slowly trying out changes to their appearance in public. Exploring support systems, both locally and online, was also an area I tried to make time for in our conversations. One person who worked in the building industry felt particularly concerned for their safety if they started the process of transitioning from male to female and so had started a "safety project" of finding at least one person in the workplace who might be understanding and able to be an ally.

In these one-off conversations, I found that the narrative skills of externalising the problem and its effects, deconstructing dominant discourses, identifying and exploring acts of survival and resistance, connecting these actions with values, and discussing support networks assisted us to connect quickly and explore new territory, contributing to a multi-storied sense of self. It was tricky to cover all these areas in a single conversation, so listening out for areas that were most relevant and checking in about this was key. Fortunately, when it came to deconstruction, I discovered that most people I was speaking to had already been thinking about the dominant messages in society and whether there were some they wanted to go along with and others they wanted to reject. As these conversations were limited to a single session, we also spoke about ways to hold on to and thicken any emerging preferred narratives. Feedback suggested that the people I was meeting with felt heard and understood.

Navigating multiple relations of power with Grace and Elizabeth

As in my work with Rose and on the phone line, when I hear stories of hurt and pain, I aim to explore the social contexts of these experiences. This helps to make visible the various discourses that have shaped not only the initial situation, but also how others have responded. For those who have been oppressed, violated or marginalised, this exploration supports them to have a voice – to name their experience in their own words. Grace and Elizabeth have agreed to share their stories with you as an illustration of ways that race, gender and sexuality can intersect to cause a complex web of discrimination. At the time I was meeting with them, Grace was visiting Sydney from Canada to spend time with her partner, Elizabeth. They had a long-distance relationship. An additional intention in visiting Sydney was to secure work, as Grace was hoping to migrate to Australia so she and Elizabeth could live together. Elizabeth had already been living in Australia for many years. Both were from Asian families.

Grace's story

In recent years, I have met with many women who work professionally in the arts, as writers, editors, actors, musicians, illustrators or animators. For some jobs, performers are required to audition in front of other applicants. Grace told me that to be hired as an actor, dancer or musician in a professional company requires not only committing your entire life to intense training and practise, but also convincing the company director that you have "that special something". This is highly subjective. There had been many times when Grace had auditioned and been told by others in attendance that she performed exceptionally well and had excellent experience, but then did not get the job.

Grace had auditioned multiple times for a company in Australia in which the existing workers were all white, and each year, those who succeeded in the auditions were also white. Was discrimination on the basis of her Korean background affecting her chances of being accepted into this company? She wondered whether it was harder to prove racism in creative industries because success is not determined simply by who is the most qualified, but by other subjective factors. Grace was troubled by this and felt a sense of hopelessness and disillusionment. She told me about a time when she had seen an Asian woman perform amazingly in a competition, and various people were convinced that she would win, but the prize was awarded to a white person who had not performed as strongly. When she shared with white colleagues her analysis that these decisions had been shaped by racism, they said something along the lines of "You are just a sore loser". When she told Black friends, they concurred with her interpretation. Grace said to me, "What does this tell you? They believe me because racism is a problem they are facing". More recently, Grace had been told by two Asian friends about their similar experiences of rejection despite performing better than the white contenders who were awarded the positions. Although she was sad for her friends, Grace felt a sense of relief at hearing this confirmation of her experience. The additional injustice of having her story dismissed had compounded the negative impact of the racism she had experienced. A couple of Grace's white colleagues did accept her conclusion. Grace said that these were people who educated themselves about social issues including racism. She felt that people who were willing to learn about racism and reflect on their own privilege would be more likely to understand that there is not an "equal playing field" in job interviews and auditions.

After Grace shared these stories, Elizabeth mentioned some acts of racism she had been subjected to growing up in Australia. As we attempted to explore and deconstruct what had been happening to Grace, the forces at play and the dominant discourses, Grace said that when people try to deny that racism is the issue, she feels powerless, and this has her spiralling down into depression. This sense of powerlessness and downward spiral was affecting her relationship with her partner. Elizabeth's view of how the world worked had been shaken. One dominant discourse that Grace and Elizabeth had been questioning was "if you work hard, you will succeed". In our conversations we examined this further. Both women stated that the meritocracy that supposedly characterises Australia, the USA and Canada does not exist. We also discussed the link between the myth of meritocracy and the spread of the self-help industry. They spoke about a sense that self-help books can have you thinking that the problem is you and is something you can fix, when actually there is a problem in the way society is operating. Grace appreciated that we were able to create space to look at the effects of these external factors on her relationship.

I learnt a lot from witnessing Grace's and Elizabeth's stories. They had me reflecting on how my race is not something I think about when I apply for a job, but that my name, my accent and my appearance all give me an advantage. I felt saddened that Grace and Elizabeth had these experiences in Australia. When I expressed this to Grace and Elizabeth and apologised for the racism they had both experienced at different times, they felt moved and acknowledged by my response. They said that it was significant to hear an apology from a white Australian.

Grace was also experiencing marginalisation in her workplace due to identifying as a lesbian. Various people had made negative comments about homosexuality and jokes about lesbians, sometimes using sexually violent and threatening language. Others laughed along or were silent. When Grace appeared upset by the sexually violent comments, fellow members of the company told her she should accept it as "just a joke". Grace's experiences were shaped by her positions as a woman, as a lesbian, and as someone subject to racism. This is an example of how multiple sites of oppression and harm can converge and compound each other, as discussed in intersectional feminism (Crenshaw, 1991). We explored ways that Grace could make a complaint, and also explored responses she had already been making to this harassment. Unable to find work in Australia, Grace returned to Canada. Having been part of these conversations with Grace about converging and intertwining sites of oppression and harm, Elizabeth chose to speak with me about some of her own experiences at work.

Elizabeth's story

Elizabeth had moved to Australia from Malaysia as a child. Like her partner, Grace, she was a talented, creative woman. She said the move had been hard at first: leaving her beloved grandmother, experiencing a new culture, and trying to make new friends.

Elizabeth felt that her voice was being silenced at work, even though she was employed to advise on creative direction. In team meetings, whenever she or Annalise, a female manager, tried to speak, they were immediately spoken over by the senior men. A clear example of her being undervalued and white privilege playing out was when the agency was creating an Asian child character who had recently migrated to Australia. Elizabeth assumed she would be invited to give some input into the development of this character, but when she suggested this, the senior men dismissed her, saying they were confident they had the ideas needed. Elizabeth and I shared an incredulous laugh. These old white men felt that they knew more about moving to Australia as a child from an Asian country than she did!

We discussed different ways Elizabeth was already responding to this situation, and looked at other steps she might consider taking. Elizabeth said it was hard to determine what actions constituted racism in her workplace as there were no other Asian people there to discuss this with, but the women would know about gender discrimination. We decided to explore ways of increasing a sense of solidarity among the women in the workplace. This was informed by the feminist principles of seeing issues as social and political rather than individual, and of formulating a collective response (Schechter, 1982). These principles underpin narrative therapy and community work.[13]

A couple of weeks later, Elizabeth told me that she had shared lunch with Annalise at a local park. Being out of the office environment freed

---

[13] The history of the connection between women meeting together in consciousness-raising groups and the philosophy and development of narrative practice was described by Cheryl White in her (2016a) piece, "Feminist challenge and women's liberation".

them up to speak openly in a way that hadn't seemed possible before. It was a wonderful conversation in which Elizabeth had been able to share her thoughts about some other talented women in the workplace who were also being undervalued, and how she felt they could encourage and draw on the talents of these women. They wondered together how they might address the silencing practices and increase the profile of women in their workplace. As the only two women in senior positions, Annalise and Elizabeth agreed that in future team meetings when either of them was interrupted, the other would point this out to the men and encourage them to listen. This solidarity would lead to a stronger voice.

One comment Annalise made during their lunch gave Elizabeth a "weird feeling". Annalise said that she thought she was employed as a manager because it looked good to have female staff when the agency was applying for arts funding. The weird feeling was telling Elizabeth that maybe she herself had been hired because she was Asian or because she was a woman or because she was a lesbian. "Am I just in the agency for token diversity, or because I am valued as a talented and creative person? What will it take for my voice to be heard and valued in the workplace?"

I used Michael White's statement of position map (2007) to further explore the impact of racism and gender discrimination with Elizabeth, mapping its effects such as "silencing", "losing hope" and "losing confidence". In this discussion, the term "injustice" emerged. Exploring the historical and current context of gender discrimination, Elizabeth shared with me some ideas about the ways women in managerial and leadership positions are treated in broader society. She mentioned the former Australian Prime Minister Julia Gillard and former US secretary of state and presidential candidate Hilary Clinton. Elizabeth noted that women in leadership positions seem to be more harshly treated by colleagues and the media than male leaders. She also noted that attacks on female leaders are often focused on their female identity. An example Elizabeth highlighted was when in 2011 the then federal opposition leader, Tony Abbott, spoke at a rally that was protesting the introduction of an emissions trading scheme with a carbon price, as proposed by Prime Minister Gillard's government. Rather than sticking to arguments about carbon pricing, the protestors brought misogynistic signs and attacked Prime Minister Gillard personally. Tony

Abbott joined the protestors and spoke in support of their actions in front of signs saying "Ditch the Witch" and "JuLiar ... Bob Brown's bitch".[14] Despite many thinking this should have been the end of Tony Abbott's political career (Massola, 2015), he was elected prime minister two years later.

Elizabeth commented that these wider events affect our daily lives. She said that when female leaders are derided in public, it condones misogyny and shapes the responses of men in the workplace. She also cited Grace's audition experiences as a turning point in seeing how the world works. "It woke me up to what is happening. Things don't operate as a meritocracy. Racism and gender discrimination make me angry." In taking a position on injustice and its effects on her, Elizabeth said, "I am finding that stepping back and noticing the political landscape and my emotional reaction is useful. It gives me clarity on how I want to respond".

In my work with Grace and Elizabeth, some sessions were conducted with both women together and some individually. Key areas of narrative practice I used with Grace and Elizabeth included:

- externalising the problem

- deconstructing dominant discourses

- supporting efforts to address injustices

- supporting collective efforts, solidarity and stronger voice through Elizabeth joining with Annalise

- supporting Grace and Elizabeth to articulate their hopes, values, skills and intentions.

They both reported finding the counselling useful. Grace noticed that Elizabeth was increasingly able to speak about her emotions, which had previously been difficult and a source of tension. Elizabeth also noticed this change. This was having a positive flow-on effect in their conversations outside the counselling room. Elizabeth said that speaking about her emotions was a new experience for her, as it did not happen in her family

---

[14] Bob Brown was leader of the Australian Greens political party and is a well-known environmental activist.

context, and that having the space in counselling to talk about things helped her form her ideas more clearly, and then gather the threads together. She noted that the threads had always been there, but she hadn't been sure how they fit together until now.

Therapeutic support guided by a collaborative and intersectional feminist framework seemed to be useful to Elizabeth. She said that she appreciated that I didn't jump in with advice, and that she appreciated my "awareness" about issues of gender, sexual identity and race: "You met me in the middle. I didn't have to educate you about these issues, and yet you didn't assume to know my experiences. You were willing to listen." As well as working towards having an awareness of important concepts and definitions, I have learnt from the people I meet with that it is important that we as practitioners ask directly about experiences of racism, discrimination or abuse based on sexual or gender identity or on disability, as it can be hard for the person holding the story to know whether we will be receptive to this information. If we are part of the dominant group, asking about these experiences lets the person know that we are willing to hear without defensiveness.

On the work front, Elizabeth noticed she felt more able to speak up, and was really pleased to have created solidarity with her colleague. This had brought her a sense of hopefulness, and she shared with me some of her visions for a more inclusive team in which she could highlight and celebrate the skills and talents of women.

****

In this chapter I have shared stories from people I have met with about social issues such as racism, homophobia and heteronormativity. I have also sought to describe the learnings I have gained over time through the generosity and patience of people who have let me into their lives. My hope is that this chapter invites you to reflect on your own work and experiences of life, to honour your learnings and those who have contributed to these learnings, and to examine areas for further development. In the next chapter I will describe additional considerations when working with people from backgrounds different to our own.

Reflection

- When you think about your work with clients,
  what is a situation that stands out to you
  as a significant learning experience?

- What was it about this situation that stands strong
  in your memory?

- What did you come to appreciate about your client
  during this period?

- What might they have come to appreciate about you?

- What did you notice about the context of your
  workplace, or of society? How did you respond?

- Was noticing or addressing this broader context part
  of your learning experience?

- Which dominant ideas are currently causing trouble
  for someone you are meeting with?

- How are you making this visible in the conversation?
  Or how might you do so?

4.

Deconstruction and concept development

This chapter offers further examples of how the deconstruction process can be used therapeutically, this time focusing on responding to violence within a family of origin or intimate relationship. I explore issues in working across cultural difference and discuss Michael White's use of Vygotsky's (1986) notion of "concept development" (M. White, 2007) to support people to move towards safer relationships after family violence. These explorations are accompanied by stories from people I have worked with who have generously agreed to share their stories. Let's start with Amirah's story.

Amirah's story

Amirah was referred for counselling due to experiencing depression and suicidal thoughts. Using the statement of position map 1 (M. White, 2007), we externalised the suicidal thoughts as something affecting her life. She had been thinking there was something inherently wrong with her, so part of our exploration included looking at the social context of the arrival of these thoughts in her life. This led to Amirah disclosing multiple stories of abuse. In the conversation below, we explored the ways men's verbal and physical abuse had affected Amirah's life. At the point in the conversation shared here, we were focusing on the ways Amirah had been treated by male relatives. We wondered together about how men are recruited into these ways of treating women and children (Jenkins, 2009; M. White, 2011). In doing this, we acknowledged that Amirah's male relatives were not the originators of these ways of thinking and of speaking to women and children. However, we both agreed that the men in her life were still responsible for their actions.

The conversation below took place a few years ago and was transcribed at that time.

Loretta: What would you call these ways your dad and brother have of speaking to you – the name calling, the put-down comments about your weight, about your worth as a person?

Amirah: Bullying ways.

Loretta: And the hitting and belting, are these also part of the bullying ways?

Amirah: Yes. He shouldn't hit me at my age – or at any age for that matter.

Loretta: He shouldn't hit you at any age.

Amirah: It's humiliating to be smacked by your dad when you are in your 30s.

Loretta: It's humiliating ... What other effects do these bullying ways of name calling, putting you down and hitting you have on you?

Amirah: They make me feel like I am nothing, and I find it hard to talk to men. If a man smiles at me on the street, I put my head down. I can't look at him.

Loretta: Are these bullying ways used on others as well?

Amirah: Yes, towards my mum. My brother's son speaks like that to his mum too. I think he learnt it from his dad.

Loretta: Are these mainly ways of speaking to women, would you say? And you've noticed your brother has been modelling it to his son too?

Amirah: Yes, I can't believe the way my nephew speaks to women, and he is only 12!

Loretta: Some of these insults your dad and brother use seem degrading to women in particular, an attack on women, such as "fat bitch" and "slut". And they imply the way women should look and behave. Have I got that right?

Amirah: Yes, you have to be thin, and you have to behave in a certain way, or you get insulted or bashed. You get harassed all the time – "Why are you eating that?"

Loretta: Sometimes I call these degrading ways of speaking to women "misogynistic", meaning the way some men speak with hatred in their language towards women. Are you familiar with this idea?

Amirah: Yeah, I'd probably call it "intimidation".

Loretta: How do you think your dad got recruited into these intimidating ways of speaking to women? What do you think influenced him?

Amirah: Maybe the culture where he was born, or maybe his parents. He has this idea: "It's my house, and you are my kids. I'll do whatever I want in my house." It's like he owns us.

Loretta: Are you seeing this idea of ownership of women and children in other people from your dad's culture or community more widely, or just in your own family? What are you noticing? Do you see it in Anglo-Australian culture too?

Amirah had noticed some aspects of Anglo-Australian culture in which women were disrespected, but she felt that some of the ideas circulating in her family were from the culture in her parents' home country. She had been noticing that there are some aspects of Australian culture in which women are not treated as equal to men.

In preparing to publish this story here, Amirah and I spoke about this again. Amirah said she had encountered expectations from some Australian men who wanted to date her that she would stay home and look after them. Amirah said that she didn't want to be treated like that: "Don't control me! Partners should encourage each other." It seemed to her that these men hadn't really been challenged about these ideas. Another contributing factor Amirah suggested was that she believed men are less likely to seek out a place to "work through their issues". In thinking about this, and about her father's experience, we wondered what stops men, or makes it harder for men, to access counselling or to speak to friends about their difficulties. Amirah named this "macho culture", describing the idea that "pride" gets in the way, and that culture, both Australian culture and many other cultures, dictates that men "can't show their emotion. They are told to suppress their emotion, but I think it would be better if they were allowed to cry".

Amirah was keen to collaborate with me on writing this chapter by giving permission for the transcript of our past conversation to be used, by updating me on what had changed since then, and by reflecting on our work together. Amirah read through the transcript and what I had written about it. We both wanted to make sure that her family members were not seen through the lens of a single story. We wanted to make clear the ways people are influenced by the attitudes they witness in the family and in society, and that attitudes and actions are shaped by these ways of viewing the world unless we are offered another view or challenged in some way. People are also shaped by their experiences. In the past year, Amirah had seen changes in her father: he had worked hard at speaking with her about his difficult experiences in life and had started to share his emotions with her. Recently he had cried in front of her. Amirah said, "I have really loved him opening up to me. I am so proud of him for showing his emotions". He was also trying to understand her children so he could be a different kind of grandfather to the way he had been a father to Amirah when she was younger.

I invited Amirah to reflect on the process of collaborating on this writing project.

> It was painful to read again about those put-downs and the hitting, but it reminded me how much I've grown and changed, and how much Dad has grown and changed. I don't know if the readers will realise how significant it was that Dad cried in front of me recently. It was so, so important. I've also realised that the last put-down was about a year ago, and I stood up for myself. I said, "Dad, you might think those words are okay or funny, but they're not okay. They make

me feel stupid, and I am not stupid". Yeah, reading this again and then talking with you, it reminds me what I've been through, and I know I am smart. I know what I've dealt with in life, and I am amazing! I also have great women friends who support me, and that is really important. Wow, yeah, I'm repeating that to you – I am amazing. I'm proud of myself and I'm going to keep on repeating that to myself, because I've never said that before. I am proud of myself!

It is important that we take care when exploring issues of violence to invite multi-storied accounts of people's families, communities, cultures and religious beliefs. As discussed by Sekneh Hammoud (publishing as Beckett, 2007) and Taimalieutu Kiwi Tamasese (2007), we need to take care that we are not colluding with stereotypes that position certain marginalised cultures as being violent, and we need to ensure that we are not assuming all people in a culture agree with ideas and practices we might consider to be oppressive. Narrative practitioners around the world inspire me with their work providing space for people of all genders to deconstruct discourses that contribute to violence and to explore acts of resistance to these discourses. It is exciting to be part of a community of practitioners with shared passions and values. These include practitioners in Palestine carefully exploring gendered discourses with women and men, while also making visible the context of living under occupation (Treatment and Rehabilitation Centre for Victims of Torture & Dulwich Centre Foundation International, 2014); Suet-Lin (Shirley) Hung's collective narrative practice deconstructing discourses around sexual violence in Hong Kong and exploring systems of power such as the court (Hung, 2011; Hung & Denborough, 2013); and Maya Sen (2019) working with young women who have been subjected to violence at the intersection of poverty and gender discourses in India.

When sharing stories of violence, people may identify some of the contributing factors as negative conclusions about women, or ideas about ownership of women and children by male relatives, or harsh and unaccepting views about LGBTQIA+ folks within the person's culture. It was not that long ago that homosexual acts were illegal in Australia, and many religious groups in Australia still have strong beliefs against people expressing their sex, sexuality or gender if it does not fit the heterocentric gender-binary model. Many folks in the LGBTQIA+ community have led the way in exposing and examining patriarchal messages in culture.

We can explore hurtful comments and actions by family and friends as being connected to *particular ideas* and trace the history of these ideas, rather than joining with the notion that ideas, comments and actions are all-encompassing of the person's culture. For example, we might ask:

- Are these ideas grounded in patriarchal or religious beliefs?

- What is the history of these ideas in this culture?

- Are these ideas as present as they once were?

- What was going on at the time when these ideas were more present/less present?

- How are these ideas supported by systems, such as the media, education and law?

When working across cultures I have found it useful to seek guidance from a colleague or supervisor from a similar background to my client to further my understanding and to support reflection and accountability in relation to the effects of my practice.

When meeting with people experiencing violence who have migrated to Australia, or who were born in Australia to migrant parents, I acknowledge any experiences of oppression and violence within their culture of origin while aiming to not make assumptions. I have not lived their experience, and I need to make sure I listen carefully. I also aim to make visible ways that Australian culture is oppressive towards women and LGBTQIA+ folks, as sometimes people who have newly migrated present a picture to me that Australia is "almost perfect". I do this by asking what they have noticed about Australian culture, for example, attitudes towards women or attitudes about violence. We might also discuss how attitudes vary throughout Australia and consider together whether there are differences in their home culture between city and country, religious and nonreligious, younger and older generations and so on.

I am also careful to ask questions that support the person to gradually stretch their understanding or articulation of concepts. In narrative practice this is called scaffolding the conversation (M. White, 2007). Its aim is to make the questions possible to answer. I think of it as using steppingstones to cross a creek, rather than trying to get across in one giant leap. We can either ask people to name the forces they see working in society, or we can offer a concept and see if it sounds familiar. In the conversation with Amirah transcribed above, I used Vygotsky's (1986) concept of "heaps" (see M. White, 2007, p. 273) to assist Amirah to name practices she had been subjected to ("name calling" and "put-down comments"), and then collected the names together to invite a group name ("bullying ways"). I also asked connecting questions to assist with what Vygotsky (1986) called thinking in "chains of association", such as "Are these bullying ways used on others as well?"[15] Vygotsky suggested that this supports "complex thinking" leading to the development of "concepts". Michael White (2007) was excited to consider what this might offer to counsellors and community workers and the people with whom we meet.

Amirah's story demonstrates how we can:

- use deconstruction to explore cultural influences on actions

- maintain that a person who uses violence is not the originator of this way of being, but is still responsible for their use of violence

- use concept development to name and explore practices of violence

- take care to bring forward multiple rather than singular stories of a person, family or culture.

In addition to practices of deconstruction and concept development, Tamasese (2007) has suggested that we invite people to share with us the liberative elements of their culture. This may include aspects of culture in which men and women are treated equally, or where women have sacred or meaningful roles. In cultures that might be described as patriarchal, we can remember that women and other marginalised folks have always resisted.

---

[15] Mark Hayward was instrumental in assisting me to articulate the links between Vygotsky's work and this conversation with Amirah.

We can draw out stories of female family members' overt or covert acts of resistance to oppressive elements of culture or find stories of famous women who have defied expectations. The person may choose to collaborate with members of their family or community to seek out lesser-known stories.

The following story from my work with Maria provides a further example of deconstruction in relation to violence when working across culture. Holding Tamasese's (2007) teachings close to me, Maria and I searched for acts of resistance to dominant cultural ideas, knowing that just because an idea is dominant does not mean it is accepted by all. In this search I aimed to connect Maria with other women in her life to reduce her sense of isolation and strengthen her sense of solidarity with other women.

Maria's story

Maria, a South American woman living in Australia, came to see me because she felt "lost" after breaking up with her boyfriend. She said it was unusual for her to be single, and she was wondering who she was outside of her relationships with men.

Maria had been in two abusive relationships with men from her own culture. "I stopped living my life. I gave up on friendships, my own hopes, and only focused on keeping him happy." We discussed what got in the way of Maria living her life and explored how controlling and emotionally abusive practices took away her sense of self-worth and agency. At one point, Maria shared with me that she thought that the reason her ex-boyfriends used control and emotional abuse was because of their "machismo" culture. Acknowledging that her home country had been colonised by Spain, we then discussed what she was noticing about the Latino culture that she described as "machismo". Maria described the ways machismo had affected her life and the lives of her female relatives. She said that ways of treating women negatively were normalised through family, friendships and soap operas. She had felt so much pressure from her former partner to fulfil a certain beauty ideal that she had undergone extensive plastic surgery. She said that Australian men were not like this, as her Australian boyfriend had not been like this. While acknowledging the awful impact of the control and emotional abuse on Maria, I was also concerned about Latino culture being written as a single story, and I wondered where Australian statistics of domestic violence fit with this idea that Australian men do not use coercive control or emotional abuse. One in every six women in Australia has experienced violence from an intimate partner or ex-partner (Australian Bureau of Statistics, 2017), and there are even greater rates of domestic violence against trans and nonbinary people (Campo & Tayton, 2015; Ussher et al., 2020). After discussing this, we deconstructed men's roles and ways of being in relationship, and questioned the idea that everyone in her community supported machismo ways of viewing women. I asked:

- Did anyone in your family know about the controlling and emotionally abusive practices that your boyfriend was using?

- Did they view it as abuse or something else?

- Was there anyone who took a stance against this sort of behaviour? Who was this? (Maria identified both her mother and grandmother – we explored each separately)

- What did she say or do?

- What values or ideas do you think she was drawing on?

- Does this mean that your mother and grandmother don't agree with these ways of treating women?

- Do you think they were the first women in your community to take a stand against this machismo culture, or do you think other women have also been doing this?

- Are there any men you know who do not go along with what you are describing as machismo culture, who choose to act differently in their relationships?

- When you left the relationship of violence, did anyone help you or support your decision?

- What did they say or do that let you know you were being supported by them to leave the violence?

- What did this support mean to you at that time?

- Do your mother and grandmother know what this support meant to you?

It became clear to both of us that many people in Maria's family and Latinx friendship network did not agree with "machismo" attitudes, and that many people had taken steps to live differently to these expectations. Maria's mother had seen the way Maria's boyfriend had been treating her, and she made it clear to Maria and to her boyfriend that she did not like this. Maria said, "Mum made a difference. She said, 'You deserve better'. My friends who are also from my culture said, 'What are you doing with him?' So I guess that shows that they think his way of treating me is not okay. But it feels normal because I see it so often". She also spoke about one of her grandmothers who encouraged the women in her family to be proud of their body shape, rather than feeling pressured to conform. Maria said, "My grandma used to tell me, 'You are beautiful the way you are'. This meant a lot to me, as it was quite different to the comments made by some other relatives".

Maria said that she liked that people in her culture were passionate, but that sometimes "jealousy" was seen as "passion", so we focused on examining and unravelling these concepts. In exploring the differences between actions shaped by passion and those shaped by jealousy, I was drawing on White's work using concept development (1995a) to build skills of discernment, encouraging Maria to articulate which actions in relationship were okay with her and which actions did not fit with how she wanted to be treated.

We spent time acknowledging the steps Maria had taken in choosing to end the two relationships that were characterised by violence. In discussing the most recent of these relationships, I asked Maria to describe actions she had taken against control, coercion and psychological abuse. The point of clarity for Maria was when physical abuse occurred. Maria said, "When he slapped me, that was it! That's when my courage came out!"

The following week, I checked in about the effects of our conversation.

Maria said, "I feel more independent after our conversation last week, remembering what I've been through and the ways I have stood up to him, like ending the relationship. It made me click – a switch turned on. I got stronger. Now, if I have a boyfriend, he will need to be *a part* of my life, not my whole life".

I was interested in what was meaningful to Maria, what made life worthwhile. Michael White's writing about this describes these values, hopes and commitments as being "absent but implicit" (M. White, 2000b) in expressions of despair, pain, anger and other strong emotions. My curiosity was piqued by Maria's expressions of having noticed that she had given up on living her life when in relationships of abuse. Some questions that were useful included:

- When you were living your life, what was it you were doing?

- Are there parts of your life you had previously enjoyed
  that you would like to take up again?

- What will you be doing when you are living your life again?

- What will your friends be noticing when you are living your life
  again in the way you want to?

- Was coming here to talk with me a step towards living your life
  again, or was it connected to another hope or value?

Here, Maria mentioned her friends quite a bit. This provided an opening to introduce re-membering practices (M. White, 2007). Because Maria had felt so "lost" after the relationship breakdown with her boyfriend, I thought it might be worth exploring her support network and the two-way contribution she and her friends made to each other's life. My intentions here were to ensure she had enough support and to further build her sense of identity.

It was a joy for me to see Maria's sense of herself, her confidence and her love of life blossom as she became more closely connected to what she wanted in life, including nurturing her friendships.

Concept development: Moving towards safer relationships

In my work with both Amirah and Maria, we found it useful to identify preferred ways of being treated in relationships. Exploring certain concepts such as "love", "trust" and "actions of care" supports people to consider which actions (their own and others) fit with these, and which transgress them. This is extraordinarily helpful when trying to differentiate between "care" and "stalking"; between "love" and "possessiveness"; between "conflict" and "abuse", for example. It helps people to consider whether they are living in accordance with their own hopes and values in the way they treat others. It helps people spot warning signs of potential abuse in the way they are treated by others. This can be very significant for people who have experienced abuse in the past, which may have shaped their concept of what love looks like, or their expectations of how a relationship works. In an interview between Michael White and Christopher McLean (M. White, 1995a), White discussed this work of naming the particularities of abuse and comparing this with specific actions that would fit with love and care. He named this as addressing "difficulties in the area of discernment" as a result of past abuse (1995a, p. 93). White described this approach or understanding as being in sharp contrast with the idea that there is something pathologically wrong with people who were abused as children or in early relationships, and that this drives the person to secretly want or seek out violent relationships. Rather than blaming the person on the receiving end of the abuse, White's approach put the responsibility back on the person who had used violence and coercive control. Once these concepts of what does and does not constitute abuse are clearer, the person is able to take a position on the actions they have been subjected to. I have found this way of working to be useful with heterosexual women and LGBTQIA+ folks who have been subjected to violence in multiple relationships.

****

In this chapter I have suggested ways of working respectfully across cultures using tools from deconstruction and concept development. It is also important to seek out consultations with practitioners from the same culture as the client or community. While Amirah was born in Australia, we deconstructed the influence of her parents' culture on the attitudes and actions of the men in her family. Maria was born in a South American country and described the impact of machismo culture on her sense of identity as she was growing up and on her relationships. In conversations with each of these women, I aimed to honour their suffering and to also make space for multi-storied accounts of their families and communities. I showed how I drew on the writing of Hammoud (publishing as Beckett, 2007) and Tamasese (2007) to ask questions about culture in ways that invite nuanced descriptions and refuse to collude with stereotypes. The stories in this chapter also demonstrated the application of Michael White's (1995a) ideas about supporting skills of discernment through concept development.

Reflection

- What stands out to you from this chapter?
  Why does this stand out?

- Is there anything you will do more of or less of on
  account of reading this chapter? What and why?

- How do you navigate cross-cultural work?
  Who has been instrumental in you learning these skills?

5.
Sharing sadness and finding glimmers of justice:
Acts of resistance and reclaiming

The women[16] with whom I meet are generally referred to me with a mental health diagnosis and a list of medications. In Australian culture, such labels invite quite negative connotations. Many of the women are also under scrutiny from child protection services. I work in generalist positions, not in the domestic violence sector, yet most of the cisgender women I have met with have been subjected to physical and/or sexual abuse, along with emotional and verbal abuse, both as children and as adults. The prevalence of this abuse tells me this is bigger than individual experience, and this has made me interested in the political context of abuse. In hearing these stories of multiple injustices, I have started searching for ways to find "glimmers of justice": recognising the women's acts of resistance and acts of reclaiming, and recognising my role in acknowledging these. This chapter explores the connection between abuse and mental distress, and ways to support people to reclaim their lives from the effects of abuse.

---

[16] This chapter is specifically focused on work I have done with cisgender women who have been subjected to violence by an intimate partner *and* sexual violence by a family member or stranger. I draw attention to the gendered experience of violence and the significantly higher number of women who are abused than men. Trans women experience even higher rates of sexual violence than cisgender women, with trans women of colour being at highest risk (Ussher et al., 2020). Nonbinary people also experience significant levels of violence. I also acknowledge that there are cultural factors that make it very difficult for men to disclose abuse.

History of a desire for justice: Honouring Simone

My desire to find justice with the women I meet with has a particular history. Several years ago, I was working with Simone in relation to the effects of childhood sexual assault and current domestic violence. A couple of months after we commenced working together, she rang me to say that she had been raped by a group of men the previous night, and to ask me to go with her to the scene with the police. It was so distressing to me to hear what had happened to her while we walked through the actual suburban street, and how she had screamed out for help and no-one came to her aid. Looking back, I wish I had realised that the fact that no-one helped Simone did not diminish her protest. I would have liked to have asked more about this protest and the intentions she had and what values this spoke to. I later went to her funeral after a medical error caused her death – another system letting her down. It took a whole year to find out what had happened.

During this time, I was concerned that domestic violence may have contributed to her death, and I protested to the coroner on Simone's behalf. Every few weeks, I made sure they knew I had not forgotten her. Considering the terrible things that had happened to her growing up, and then the ongoing violence from her partner, the sexual assault by strangers and the death resulting from a medical mistake, it was hard to hold all this in my mind. Whenever I drove past her street, I felt sick and fearful. I feel glad that I have learnt different ways of supporting women. When I support women in recognising misogyny and moving away from its effects, I am honouring Simone. When I assist women to acknowledge the protests they have made and are making against abuse, and I am an audience honouring their protests, I am also honouring Simone's protests. Re-membering (Myerhoff, 1982, 1986; M. White, 2007) Simone is quite moving for me, and mirrors the way I hope to work in assisting people to find historical links to their values and the ways they are currently acting in line with these values.

In this chapter I describe nine key themes that guide my practice[17]:

- sharing sorrow, demonstrating that I am not afraid
  of difficult stories and building trust

- richly acknowledging the effects of abuse

- acknowledging the political context of experiences
  and expressions of distress and deconstructing pathology

- rebuilding identity – re-membering

- double listening

- noticing responses as acts of resistance at the time of abuse

- acknowledging resistances in the present

- highlighting acts of resistance as political action:
  finding glimmers of justice

- outsider-witnessing practices.

I hope that each of these themes, in some small way, honours Simone.

Sharing sorrow, demonstrating that I am not afraid of difficult stories and building trust

The women I meet with have experienced many difficulties in their lives as a result of abuse. Such difficulties include fear of leaving the house, trouble falling asleep at night, nightmares, fear of crowded places, self-hate, guilt for being alive, self-harm, suicidal thoughts, anorexia and bulimia. Some have used drugs in the past, either to alleviate the pain of the distress brought by abuse, or due to coercion by the person enacting the abuse. The women live with the continuing impact of this previous drug use on their lives, including

---

[17] The narrative practices described in this chapter would be relevant to work with people of all genders.

removal of their children by child protection services or by concerned family, monitoring and judgement by family and community, disconnection from friends who are still involved with drugs, the daily requirement to pick up methadone from the chemist, and diseases such as hepatitis C.

Some women who come to meet with me fear that their stories are "too bad", and that I won't want to hear about the abuse and its effects. They worry that the issues are "too complicated", and that I will refer them to other services. Some women, when attending counselling elsewhere, have been stopped part-way through a story and referred to a specialist service, such as sexual assault counselling. This has sometimes inadvertently confirmed the idea that their story was too hard to hear or that they have "too many problems". In my work it is therefore important in building trust and connection to demonstrate my willingness to hear such difficult stories.

One woman said to me that she likes that I ask more questions when she says something about cutting or suicidal thoughts. She said this shows her I'm not scared to ask, I am interested, and that it is okay to speak about these things. She spoke about another worker simply asking, "Are you safe tonight?", and then moving on to another topic when she assured them she was "safe". This had her thinking that people are sometimes not comfortable with hearing about self-harm or suicidal thoughts, and this added to the silencing she already experienced in relation to the abuse. Demonstrating a willingness to listen helped establish a relationship of trust, which allowed her to tell me about the abuse she had experienced. It is also a political stance on my behalf to refuse to collude with silencing.

When listening to people who are experiencing self-harm, suicidal thoughts or food issues, I pay special attention to their experience and use their own words in my questions. I try not to make assumptions or jump in with my own ideas, just because I know something about these issues or even because I've discussed them with this person before. I've noticed that self-harm, suicidal thoughts and anorexia/bulimia can change their tactics often, especially when certain tactics have been exposed to the light and the person is getting clearer on how to get around that tactic. These problems really work hard at attacking people's identities, hopes and values. Part of my practice of accountability to the people I meet with is to make space available for hearing these thoughts and examining their tactics so that we both know what the person is being subjected to. This way, we can work on it together so that there is a sense of solidarity, rather than the person feeling on their own with the distress.

When listening to stories of self-harm or suicidal thoughts, I try to focus my listening on really hearing the pain the person is expressing, and not getting distracted by worker anxiety (Stout, 2010). This can be difficult when the person's safety seems to be at risk. When anxiety tries to get the better of me and I feel uncertain about how to proceed, I use a support team available to my mind (Pederson, 2014). I think of therapists I know well and whom I trust. I imagine what they might notice in the story, or what they might be curious about. Once I've done this, ideas for questions suddenly pop into my mind. I particularly focus on the alternative story of how the person has got through dark thoughts before, and how they have made the effort to speak with me today. This privileges the person's skills and knowledges, rather than relying only on professional knowledge. Often, these skills, such as finding safe places to rest, building a support network, using distraction or finding comfort through music, have been overlooked or diminished by others. This is similar to the experience of disregard or diminishment often experienced by people when speaking of their responses to abuse. In both of these situations, this disregard can result in shaming, despair and self-hate.

Another way to build trust and maintain safety for the person I'm meeting with is respecting the person's choice about whether or not they want to discuss the assault. I assure the person that we can work together on reducing the impact of the effects of the assault without discussing the details (M. White, 1995a). This reduces the risk of retraumatising the person. It is also a way of being decentred. I check whether it is me or another person they wish to speak with about the assault. As well as respecting choice, this is an attempt to avoid replicating the work of others or accidentally getting the person to tell their story repeatedly, especially as some of the people I see also have a mental health worker involved.

Richly acknowledging the effects of abuse

Many of the women I meet with have experienced multiple assaults from various people both in childhood and in adulthood. Often, attempts to speak out have been met in silencing ways, such as denial that the abuse occurred, dismissal of the seriousness of the effects of the abuse, demands to keep quiet to avoid shame on the family, and blaming the person who was subjected to the abuse. This leads to confusion, shame and the construction of negative identity conclusions. In telling the women I believe them, and expressing my genuine sorrow about what happened, I am sometimes the first person, or one of a small group, to express care about what the person has experienced.

Mary was referred for counselling because she was experiencing suicidal thoughts. She said that at times she wanted to escape this world, and the thoughts told her to take her child with her. Mary finally broke the silence about being sexually assaulted by a family member by speaking to another family member about it. His response was, "Yeah, well, that's what happens. It happened to me. I got over it. It's no big deal". While he believed her, she experienced this response as extremely dismissive, uncaring and silencing of further discussion. When people describe to me such minimisation of abuse and its effects, I find these questions helpful:

- What effect did this response have on you?

- What meaning did you take from this response?

- Did this response make it harder to speak to others about the abuse?

- How have you been able to try again and speak to me or to others? What did it take?

- What would you call this action? "Speaking out", "standing against silencing" or perhaps something else?

- What does this say about what is important to you that you were willing to "speak out" despite the steps the person who abused you took to silence you, and then the continuation of this silencing by the person you tried to tell?

- Instead of the response you received initially, what would you have liked them to say or do? If they had responded in a more acknowledging way, what would that have looked like?

These questions also provide possible openings to acknowledge the political context of community responses to abuse.

My expression of sadness over what happened to Mary, and the exploration of what sort of response she would have preferred, supported her to then tell other women about the abuse at a group facilitated by another service. The women were moved to tears, which Mary experienced as very acknowledging. Some women were then able to speak of their own experiences of abuse. Mary said she was pleased and comforted by this two-way contribution, and she continued connecting with one of the women after the group finished.

Richly acknowledging the effects of abuse is not a one-off event. Sometimes, people revisit stories I have already heard. My willingness to return to old stories is another way to contribute to a rich description of the effects of the abuse. It's also an opportunity to further deconstruct dominant ideas or to further investigate the tactics of the problem. Looking for entry points to the alternative story, such as skills they used to survive, values held on to in the face of difficulties, and acts of care for others, ensures that in each retelling there is opportunity for further double-story development. This allows for more meaning-making to occur, and for a thickening of the preferred identity the person is stepping into.

Acknowledging the political context of experiences and expressions of distress and deconstructing pathology

Tahlia was a young parent who inspired me through her determination to live life differently, and to parent her child differently from how Tahlia herself had been parented. Tahlia had experienced multiple and ongoing abuses, both as a child and an adult, which had serious consequences for her life and for her identity. She was referred to me by our state child protection service. They did not hold concerns about Tahlia's care of her daughter, but had a continued presence in her life as Tahlia had been a "ward of the state" and due to recent intimate partner violence.

Tahlia and I developed a rich description of the effects of the abuse. Michael White (1995a) wrote about the importance of recognising that the meaning people make from events of abuse can create negative identity conclusions that lead to actions against the self. Actions against the self are often then viewed by the person as confirming that they are indeed worthless or deserving of abuse. Narrative practices such as re-authoring, deconstructing, searching for the absent but implicit, and noticing acts of resistance (M. White, 2000b) provide us with the opportunity to assist those we meet with to reconsider the meaning that's been made of the abuse. For Tahlia, the meaning made of the multiple acts of childhood abuse against her was that "nobody wants me", leading to the identity conclusion "I am unlovable". She was also influenced by ideas of genetics and familial environment, and by being labelled as having borderline personality disorder (BPD): "Whether it is nature or nurture, I'm destined to hurt people".

When Tahlia came to meet with me, she had been struggling with what she referred to as "cutting". Tahlia experienced self-harm in different ways at different times – as an expression of distress, as an attempt to reconnect to feeling when distress had left her numb, and as an act of protest. This fits with the experience noticed by others (Favazza, 2011). Tahlia did not want cutting for her life. While she honoured her scars as testimony to all she had been through, she did not want her daughter to see fresh scars. She was also concerned that cutting might be interpreted by her child protection worker as "proof that I'm crazy or unstable" and that they might take her child away from her. She was worried that if she spoke about the suicidal thoughts she was experiencing, she would be hospitalised, and that this would lead to removal of her child.

Acknowledging the context of experiences and expressions of distress is a significant part of my work. Sexual or physical abuse increases the likelihood that people will experience repetitive self-harm (Favazza, 2011). Noticing the link between abuse and actions against the self assists me to see these as expressions of distress, rather than symptoms of mental illness (Lee & Pederson, 2014).

The externalising conversations map, also known as statement of position map 1 (M. White, 2007), was useful in exploring the context of what had been happening for Tahlia in the lead up to the cutting. Tahlia said there were connections to past abuse and also a current situation of emotional abuse. The most common lead up to cutting was critical comments by members of her foster family about her parenting and her identity: "You're borderline, so you are going to hurt your daughter, just like your parents hurt you and your brother." The distress she experienced due to the multiple abuses and injustices had been interpreted by mental health professionals as borderline personality disorder, and Tahlia had told me that this was regularly used by her foster family to put down her parenting, and to make negative predictions about her future. She described these hurtful comments as being "like razor blades raining down on me". Through further exploring the impact of this, we were able to acknowledge the link to suicidal thoughts, as these comments attacked her identity as a parent and therefore attacked her hope for the future. Towards the end of my work with Tahlia, her foster mother became seriously ill, and this was a turning point in their relationship. Tahlia's foster mother became open to noticing Tahlia's acts of care towards her and the family, and this changed her ideas about Tahlia. She in turn demonstrated acts of care towards Tahlia, and their relationship moved towards "closeness", which was their preferred direction.

Our work together gave Tahlia a safe space to find ways to decrease the cutting, and find ways through the suicidal thoughts without fear of being seen as an "unfit mother". Using externalising conversations, we were able to separate the problems Tahlia experienced from her sense of self, and we noticed the intentions cutting and suicidal thoughts had for life. By naming these problems as an outcome of the emotional and physical abuse and the sexual assaults, we moved away from an individualised and pathologised description of her experience of self-harm and suicidal thoughts and towards an acknowledgment of the political context of the abuse.

The effects of trauma on Tahlia's life had led to her being given various mental health diagnoses, which had convinced her that she was "damaged". This affected her hopes for her life and the life of her child. We deconstructed these labels, but as she consulted a psychiatrist for medication, and was on the waiting list for a service for people with borderline personality disorder, it was difficult to maintain long-term separation from these labels. Feminist writers have illustrated how, throughout Western history, women who have become distressed by the abuse they have experienced have been more likely than men to have this distress diagnosed and treated as a mental illness (Chesler, 1972). Expressions of outrage over abuse, such as distancing oneself from family, heavy alcohol or drug use, or practices of self-harm, do not fit with dominant ideas of "ladylike behaviour". This rush to diagnose and categorise means that many women are having their expressions of distress in relation to injustice labelled as mental illness.

I've been thinking a lot about the unfairness of calling the trauma resulting from abuse "mental illness". This shifts the focus and responsibility away from the person who abused and makes invisible the influence of patriarchal values on the occurrence of abuse. Many of the women I meet with have been under scrutiny. The focus of services is often on mothers – either on their "failure" to leave a violent situation, or on expressions of distress that are viewed as mental illness. Mental illness is seen in Western culture as an individual problem, and it is often viewed as pathology caused by genetics. What injustices do these labels make invisible? What impact on worker attitudes do labels like BPD have when they are documented in referrals? What effects do these labels have on the ways women see themselves? Rather than diagnosing self-harm, suicidal thoughts and eating disorders as mental illnesses, I choose instead to see them as expressions of distress that make sense in our culture and in the context of abuse and injustice.

Unmasking the operations of problems like self-harm and suicidal thoughts and deconstructing patriarchy are political aspects of my work.[18] In making visible the link between these problems and abuse, we are locating the problem as a social and political responsibility, not as an individual failure.[19]

---

[18] I'm quite concerned that even experience-near names for problems may obscure the politics of a person's experience if the context is not examined (M. White, 1995a). For example, renaming self-harm as "cutting" doesn't demonstrate that it is an outcome of abuse, and that the abuse was enabled through social attitudes and systems. If we don't examine the context of the problems women experience, we may inadvertently contribute to the pathologising of women's distress.

[19] I appreciate McPhie and Chaffey's (2000, pp. 38–43) deconstruction of some dominant ideas about women who have been abused and their questioning about who benefits from these ideas.

The following questions (shaped by Tahlia's responses) assisted us to make these links:

- Who encouraged the shame that you experienced in relation to the abuse?

- How did this person trick you into believing what shame had to say?

- This shame that was put on you by this man's abusive words and actions, what did it get you thinking about yourself?

- So the shame invited thoughts of worthlessness and got you hating yourself. Did this sense of worthlessness and self-hate get you doing anything or stop you from doing things?

- It got you cutting yourself, caused all sorts of trouble with food, and made it hard for you to leave the house? So these things you've been struggling with over the past few years started because of the abuse and the shame that was put on you. Have I got that right?

- Have you noticed before now that the cutting, the problems with food and the difficulty leaving the house were pushed on to your life by the abuse, or is this a new consideration?

- What is it like noticing this link?

- What has noticing the beginnings of these struggles got you thinking about the idea you've been carrying that these problems are your own fault, and that they are proof that you are "mentally ill"?

- Who has been benefiting by blaming you for these struggles you've been facing?

When discussing the purpose of deconstruction in therapy, Michael White used the ideas of Bourdieu (1988) in saying that "we might become more aware of the extent to which certain 'modes of life and thought' shape our existence, and that we might then be in a position to choose to live by other 'modes of thought'" (M. White, 1992, p. 122). In deconstructing the messages of patriarchy, I am attempting to increase awareness of the influence of the systems we are living within, and the impact of these on the shaping of our identities and actions. I am hoping that the people I work with are able to further separate their identities from the problems in their lives, and consider whether the "modes of thought" influenced by patriarchy fit with their own values, hopes and purposes or not. I hope they will be freer to live their lives the way they choose, rather than according to what is insidiously imposed on them.

An example of this deconstruction is noticing and examining the link between misogynistic verbal abuse, or the emotional abuse that happens alongside physical or sexual abuse, and the words that are present in the woman's thoughts during practices of self-harm, such as "you are worthless and stupid" or "you deserve to be punished". When the words of abuse are recognised as being similar to the words of the problem, they can be seen as being an outcome of the abuse. This provides more possibilities for questioning the intention of what self-harm or anorexia/bulimia (or a more experience-near name) might want for the person's life, and whether these intentions fit with the person's intentions (Maisel et al., 2004).

Here are some examples of questions that start with exploring the effects of the problem and then make the link with abuse:

- When did the thoughts about self-harm first start?

- Is this when actions of self-harm started too, or was that later?

- What was happening for you at those times at home? At school?

- Do certain words or thoughts come into your mind just before self-harm happens, or while it is happening?

- Are these words familiar to you? Have you heard them from someone else in your life?

My passion about asking questions that deconstruct patriarchal messages and systems is shaped by my own values and principles, which have been shaped by my relationships and experiences, and by the meanings I have made from those experiences. I need to be careful that my passion does not tip over into being "centred" in this work. I am deliberately influential, however, as I feel ethically required to assist people to examine the contexts of their lives, and to notice their influence on the problem story (M. White, 1997). During my conversations, I carefully check with people about whether these questions and ideas are of interest to them or not, and how they might let me know if I were taking the conversation into territory they were not interested in or felt uncomfortable to discuss. So far, all of the women I've met with have been very interested in these ideas and have been making their own observations of society and relationships, but have not necessarily had the opportunity to put these observations into words before. Tahlia was quite interested in discussing issues of patriarchy, including the use of misogynistic language by her male friends. Her own noticings about society, and her interest in examining these issues, influenced our work together.

Rebuilding identity: Re-membering

When I meet with people who experience suicidal thoughts, I am conscious of building a support team. However, in Tahlia's situation, this was complex. Fear made it hard for Tahlia to trust people, or to engage in conversations with other parents in our groups. When involving others in therapy proves difficult, sometimes re-membering conversations about significant others can be influential (M. White, 2007), offering exploration of two-way contribution. Holding re-membering conversations in my work with Tahlia was also tricky, however, due to the abusive aspects of many of her relationships. For instance, we discovered unique outcomes, like when adults in her life assisted her after an assault (when she was a toddler) or tried to protect her from her parents, and we considered what this care might suggest they valued in her or in their relationship with her. This picture was then complicated, however, by the sense of betrayal Tahlia experienced, as it appeared that these adults did not take action to prevent further abuse, and this resulted in the death of her baby brother, Kane, and placement of Tahlia into foster care where further abuse occurred. Over time, I realised that re-membering conversations in relation to her brother might be significant to Tahlia.

Tahlia had been told that unless she could cry about the death of her brother, she would never "get well". After deconstructing these dominant ideas of grieving and healing, we discussed ways she remembered and honoured him. She said that every year on his birthday she bought a cake, celebrating his birthday by herself. Tahlia thought of him often, but on the anniversary of Kane's death, she dedicated the whole day to thinking about him. We wondered together what Kane might say about Tahlia remembering him, and about what he might say about her getting through tough times. His voice was encouraging to her. We also wondered whether this demonstrated her love for him. This was particularly significant because Tahlia at times had been recruited into the idea that her BPD diagnosis meant that she was incapable of love. I was hoping that through evaluating these initiatives, and what they reflected about what was important to her, Tahlia would develop an appreciation of the initiatives and a renewed sense of personal agency (M. White, 2004a).

I wondered if it might be possible to consider what Tahlia had contributed to Kane's life, and asked the following questions:

- I imagine there were some scary times for you both. What might have been some ways that you comforted Kane? Do you think perhaps you stood by his cot so he knew he was not alone? Or maybe you passed him a toy or a dummy?

- What might it have been like for Kane to know you were there, and that you loved him and wanted him to be comforted?

- There were times when your parents didn't attend to your needs or Kane's needs. What do you think it was like for him to have a sister who noticed him and loved him?

- What do you think it might have suggested to him about his own worth that you noticed him and loved him?

- If he were here to see the way you attend to your daughter's needs when she is hungry or wet, what might he appreciate about your parenting?

- If he knew about the way you have kept your daughter away from the violent anger of her dad, what might he say about your efforts to give her a different life to the one you and Kane had?

- If Kane were here right now, what is your guess about what he'd say it means to him that you remember him, and that you wish things had been different for the two of you?

- What might he think the anger and sadness you feel about his death suggests is important to you?

The re-membering conversation we engaged in brought out very moving stories of Tahlia's love for her baby brother, and the care and comfort she gave him. I got to hear about his "mischievous smile" and the way he would lean into her when going to sleep, and her guess about what this "leaning in" might mean. She smiled as she described him to me. She said that this was the first time she had spoken in detail about him as a person to anyone. Usually, she had just referenced his death, but never spoke of his life. Tahlia said she really appreciated this about our discussion.

Double listening

The ways Tahlia distracted her baby brother, keeping him quiet to help him avoid physical abuse by their parents, and the way she attended to him during times of extreme neglect, spoke of her responses to the trauma they were both subjected to. I am so relieved to know about double listening (M. White, 2004b) so that I can not only listen to the accounts of traumatic events and the distress that abuse brings, but also ask about the skills and knowledges people have used to get through, and the values linked to this. I particularly noticed this in Angel Yuen's discussion of second-story development:

The second story also acknowledges that, even though a child may not have been able to stop a traumatic event, which may have involved a range of abuses, or had no control over events of suffering such as disease or death, ample possibility still remains to co-discover how they have responded to these events in many ways. (Yuen, 2007, p. 6)

Questions can be asked about responses at the time of the abuse and its immediate aftermath, or about responses to the ongoing effects of abuse. Using concepts from the re-authoring conversations map (M. White, 2007), questions can allow the person's own responses to the abuse to become more richly known and acknowledged, assisting the person to view themselves differently and have an increased sense of agency (Denborough & Preventing Prisoner Rape Project, 2005; M. White, 2004b; Yuen, 2007).

During my year of meeting with Tahlia, she was subjected to a violent rape by a man she was dating, and her life was threatened. The safety we had established in the therapeutic relationship allowed her to speak about this assault. Response-based questions generally fit under the following categories, and are shaped by the person's answers to the questions (in this example, the questions were shaped by Tahlia's answers):

Landscape of action

- Even though you couldn't stop him from raping you, in what ways were you trying to protect yourself or lessen the harm?

Landscape of identity

- In changing from screaming to crying silently, what was your intention?

- What did you know or guess about crying silently that suggested it could help you be a bit safer?

- So it stopped him from killing you? Would you call this a skill of survival then or something else?

The history of this skill (landscape of action)

- Is crying silently something you are familiar with? Has this helped you in the past?

Tahlia told me that she had learnt as a young child that crying silently can be safer than screaming – crying loudly in response to beatings from her parents increased the intensity of the beatings. Other landscape of identity questions seek to identify the values these actions and skills are linked to.

Noticing responses as acts of resistance at the time of abuse

In my conversations with women who have experienced abuse, their stories always include actions for survival, whether these are overt attempts to fight off the person assaulting them (choking him, punching him), or ways to lessen the harm (recognising when fighting is bringing stronger harm and becoming still or quiet to survive), or ways of trying to get help (screaming for help, writing stories at school about the abuse). These can be linked to valuing their own life, or needing to protect their child whom they love and whose life they treasure. My experiences of these conversations support over and again White's (2004b) analysis that people always respond to the traumatic events of their lives:

> People always take steps to try to prevent the trauma, and even if preventing the trauma is clearly impossible, they take steps in efforts to preserve what is precious to them. Even in the face of overwhelming trauma, people take steps to try to protect and preserve what they give value to. (M. White, 2004b, p. 48)

Acknowledging resistances in the present

As a result of the distress Tahlia felt over the rape, she had cut the words "Please stop" into her body. Rather than responding from a place of worker anxiety about the cutting, I used double listening (M. White, 2004b), which allowed me to hear her pain and distress (Stout, 2010), acknowledge the protest implicit in the words she cut, and assist her to find other ways to express this distress. Narrative positioning allowed me to also express sadness and outrage about the rape, and sadness that she had been so distressed as to cut words into her body.

Prior to the most recent sexual assault, Tahlia had already been struggling with fear and suicidal thoughts as a result of previous abuse. When I asked her about the impact of looking at her responses and thinking about ways she was reclaiming her life, Tahlia said:

> Coming here after the rape was helpful because I wasn't afraid to talk to you. I can see that I was definitely fighting for my life on that night. I didn't want that to be my last breath. This shows me that I wanted to live. I know that I'm not worthless. I'm struggling, but I'm not worthless. I need to live.

Highlighting acts of resistance as political action: Finding glimmers of justice

Dominant culture has a key role in the construction and continuation of problems (Handsaker, 2012). In discussing his use of the phrase "subordinate stories", Michael White (in M. White & Epston, 1990) referred to Foucault's (1980) ideas on dominant and subordinate knowledge, and pointed out that stories are not subordinated by chance, but as a result of the operations of power. These ideas got me thinking about how women's stories of resistance to sexual or physical assault can be hidden or overlooked, and that highlighting acts of resistance is political action. In turn, this has led me to considerations of justice for women who have been subjected to abuse.

In my conversations with women, the topic of justice often comes up. Most do not believe justice in the traditional sense is available for them. For example, Sarah said, "You can't rely on the courts for justice. It's not set up for justice for women. It is very hard for children or women to speak up at all". One woman, who was sexually assaulted as a child, believed she did not get justice because her father was sent to "rehabilitative counselling" rather than prison after a two-year court process. When considering taking a recent assault by another person to court, she was told the cross-examination would be difficult because she would not be considered a "credible witness" due to her history of sexual assault and the resulting "mental illness" she was experiencing before the rape. She asked me a very moving question: "Does this mean that once someone has been sexually abused as a child, society allows them to be raped throughout their adult life, and no-one will be held to account?"

The community attitudes that make it hard to tell friends about sexual abuse or assaults are also prevalent in health services and the police, although some improvements have occurred. I hold Simone's story in my mind when responding to women after a sexual assault. After being gang-raped, she was asked by a sexual assault counsellor, "Why were you walking at night?" Simone took this question to be implying that she was stupid and partly responsible. The responsibility was not placed with the men who raped her. Together with the women I'm meeting with, I have had to come up with some alternative types of justice (Hung & Denborough, 2013). We have been looking at efforts to address the effects of abuse as acts of reclaiming life and discussing whether these are "glimmers of justice".

Just as we can acknowledge acts of resistance at the time of the abuse, so too can we notice acts of resistance that occur after the abuse has taken place, and/or acts of reclaiming life from the longer-term effects of the abuse. Any of these acts of reclamation can be recognised and linked to considerations of justice (Hung & Denborough, 2013). Let me offer some examples.

One woman described that during a sexual assault by her close friend, she choked him to try to make him stop, even though he had drugged her. In the following weeks, he kept trying to contact her. However, she told me she was deliberately *not* changing her phone number. She said, "He is a very scary guy. No-one ever stands up to him. By not changing my number, I'm standing up to his intimidation. By ignoring his calls and texts, I'm showing him I'm not scared".

Tahlia has also taken action to reclaim her life from fear. Fear had been very strong in Tahlia's life, making it hard for her to leave the house. Therefore, every time she left the house to do something for herself or her daughter, she was reclaiming her life from the effects of abuse. She said that this was linked to her valuing of her daughter's life, and her hope that her daughter would have a better life than Tahlia had as a child. In striving to finish her education and get a job working with animals, Tahlia hoped to link her love of animals to her desire to show the people who had hurt her that they had not stopped her reaching her dreams. She also wanted to show society that people with a BPD label can be "productive members of society". In her efforts to care for her daughter, she said she was trying to show the people who hurt her, and society, that just because someone has been abused, it does not mean that they will go on to abuse others.

Sarah and I spoke about ways she had reclaimed her life from bulimia, which started after she was sexually assaulted as a teenager. We also spoke about how she had reclaimed her life from the anger, which was getting her to do things that didn't fit with her values. She stated that forgiving others, not going back to the bulimia, and loving and protecting her children were ways that she was doing what she wanted with her life: "I'm reclaiming my life by not going back down the path of bulimia. I'm under so much stress right now, and my daughter's father tells me I'm fat … but I can't go back to bulimia. I have a better life now, and I want to keep this better life for my kids."

We then discussed the link between the bulimia and the sexual abuse. I asked, "Since the bulimia started as an effect of the abuse, does it mean that by standing up to the bulimia, you are standing up to the effects of the abuse?" Sarah agreed and seemed excited by the idea that she was standing up to the abuse and reclaiming her life, and that I was recognising these stands. I asked, "Would you call this a 'reclaiming' or a 'certain type of justice' or something else?"

Sarah said, "Both! I'm reclaiming my life, and this is a type of justice. Not the court type, but still, I'm living my life the way I want."

These considerations of linking women's acts of reclamation to ideas about justice can be further explored. What difference would it make to our conversations if women's resistance to injustice and the effects of abuse were acknowledged as efforts to achieve "glimmers of justice"?

In exploring these realms, I have regularly noticed in my practice that women can more easily connect with a sense of justice or care for others than for themselves. This notion of care and justice for others can be significant to build on and to use as a scaffold in conversations about justice. For instance, I have started to use questions that invite the person to speak in the third person:

- If this happened to your friend – if your friend were raped when she was drunk – who would you hold responsible for the assault?

- What would you want to say to your friend about the assault that she had been subjected to?

In the future, I will continue to explore ways of linking women's acts of reclamation with acts of justice-seeking. I'll also continue to explore how women's friendships might richly support considerations of justice for self as well as justice for others. The involvement of friends and other workers as outsider witnesses might also be significant.

Outsider-witnessing practices

The abuse had a significant effect that Tahlia wished to change: she felt disconnected from her feelings, and sometimes this had her doubting her own existence. Her words reminded me of the words of Barbara Myerhoff (1982, p. 233): "Unless we exist in the eyes of others, we may come to doubt even our own existence. Being is a social, psychological construct, made, not given". Myerhoff's words made me consider Tahlia's isolation from caring relationships and the effects of the "critical comments" she was being subjected to. This got me thinking of the importance of some sort of outsider-witnessing process (M. White, 2007). I recruited outsider witnesses when sharing Tahlia's story with other professionals (Lee & Pederson, 2014), and gathered responses using White's four categories of enquiry (M. White, 2007) to share back with her. Tahlia had said to me, "My biggest hope is to share my story and give people hope". The responses the witnesses offered back to Tahlia demonstrated that she had indeed given people hope for their work and also hope in their personal journeys.

How this way of working affects me

There are many reasons I like working in this way. Recognising patriarchy and misogyny in this work not only reduces shame, but also opens possibilities for finding ways other than self-harm to express anger and protest. At the same time, not only does double listening address my concerns about not retraumatising people, but through supporting them to find a safe place to stand (M. White, 2004b), I am also finding a safe place myself. I have heard from people I meet with, and seen in their changed body language, that this way of discussing trauma is new for them, and much more positive in its effects than other experiences they have had of discussing their history. I love assisting people to see themselves in a preferred light. Listening for responses, skills, values and hopes is much less distressing for me than only paying attention to the traumatic events and their effects. This helps me to stay in this work long-term.

Even though I notice these acts of resistance, at times I still experience significant sadness about the sheer number of assaults I hear about from the small number of women with whom I meet. After a day of hearing stories of men's abuse of women, I take particular care to call into my mind stories of men I know personally, or have heard of, who have put thought and effort into deconstructing dominant ways of viewing and treating women. I remember acts of care and gentleness by these men. This helps me keep going in this work and helps me hold on to hope for society.

Focusing on reclamation and alternative ideas of justice, and seeing this as political, has brought me a stronger sense of purpose in my work, and increased hopefulness about upcoming sessions. I have a sense of joy when we uncover together some steps towards glimmers of justice. This sometimes involves highlighting the women's stories of reclaiming to the child protection workers involved with their families. A service I worked with designed a template for writing reports to our state child protection service that includes a section to record a family's skills and knowledges, and another section for the family's hopes for the future. These documents are written in collaboration with the family, and they can read the report before it is sent to the child protection service. This way of working has assisted in altering the child protection workers' views of the families, and has led to a more collaborative approach between services and with the families.

Collecting, archiving and sharing acts of reclaiming makes me feel that as women we are joined, and we are stronger together. We are stronger when we share in sadness. We are stronger when we share anger and action. I feel inspired by the women's efforts, and this pushes me to continue noticing steps of reclamation. Keeping this in the forefront of my mind assists in my next conversations.

****

In this chapter I have raised the idea that recognising the effects of abuse on problems such as self-harm, suicidal thoughts and anorexia/bulimia can be a political aspect of therapeutic work. Examining the messages and systems of patriarchy, which allow abuse to continue, and which make it hard for those who have been abused to speak about the abuse, moves these problems from an individual to a social arena, reducing the pathologising of women's distress. This draws on the feminist ideas discussed in earlier chapters. Noticing acts of reclaiming life as "glimmers of justice" has been experienced as helpful by the women I meet with and supports me in continuing with this work. My hope is that in reading these stories, you will feel invited to consider the acts of resistance to assault and acts of reclaiming of life that the people you are meeting with have taken and consider how you can thicken these subordinated stories so they don't slip back into the forgotten or unknown.

In the next chapter, the focus is on re-engaging with history through a feminist lens, and using current affairs and social media to explore and expand on the connections between the experiences of the people we meet with and broader movements such as #MeToo.

Reflection

- Are you willing to listen to the hard stories?

- If not, what gets in the way? Is this something you want to work towards addressing?

- In what ways (verbal and nonverbal) are you communicating your willingness or unwillingness to listen to difficult stories?

- When the injustices faced by the people you meet with bring a heaviness or sense of overwhelm, how do you respond? Is there an idea that helps reposition you? Is there a group of friends or colleagues you join with for a sense of solidarity?

- How might you help newly acknowledged acts of resistance or reclaiming to stay visible after the sessions ends?

6.
A feminist re-engagement with history

An understanding of the politics of experience can help to undermine the shame and self-blame that often accompany experiences of family[20] and domestic violence, sexual assault and harassment (M. White, 1995a). Bringing a feminist lens to our re-examinations of past events can elicit transformative new understandings that unsettle previous assumptions and allow new stories to emerge from the shadows of memory. This chapter shares stories from my work with Elle. We used deconstruction questions to reconsider experiences of violence, harassment and coercion from a feminist perspective. Deconstruction questions enable people to locate experiences and responses in time to explore cultural attitudes and historical contexts. Situating events in time and place, rather than having them dislocated from context, provides opportunities to re-engage with history and create new perspectives, knowledge and connections. This chapter also shows how Elle and I drew on news reports and podcasts about current events to further explore context and collective experiences. This included reflection about the #MeToo movement, which Elle found resonant and inspiring.

---

[20] Here I use the term "family violence" to refer to violence from one sibling towards another or from a young person towards their parent.

Elle's story

In previous conversations, Elle and I had explored internalised homophobia and the social forces at play in this. We had also discussed ageism and the particular pressure it exerts on women. These conversations of deconstruction (see Chapter 4) led to re-authoring conversations (M. White, 2007) about Elle's skills and values. Today, while further discussing what had shaped Elle's hopes, values and intentions, a story about surviving family violence emerged. Elle stated, "We don't need to talk about the violence – I've already talked all that through with another therapist". This was a reminder for me not to ask about the details of the acts of violence, both to avoid retraumatising Elle, and to respect her signal that she did not want to discuss it again. I was curious, though, about the *meaning* Elle had made of the experience of violence, and how this meaning might be influencing her life and relationships, her hopes and intentions. This curiosity was informed by social constructivist ideas in narrative practice that have shaped my understanding of identity formation and the affect this has on the actions people take in life (M. White, 2004b). Elle felt that she had not been protected from her brother's use of violence towards herself and her mother, Joy. She said with strength in her voice, and something that sounded like anger and determination, "Mum was powerless at that time. I decided I was never going to be like her. She couldn't assert authority".

This had me wondering if I might open space for "something else" in Elle's recounting of history to help scaffold from "the known and familiar" story of Joy's powerlessness, or failure to protect, to "something possible to know" (Vygotsky, 1986; M. White, 2007, p. 271). I didn't know where this conversation would take us, but I held some assumptions key to narrative practice: that people's lives are multi-storied (M. White, 2004b); that social and political contexts influence people's understandings, experiences and options (M. White, 2004b); and that people who seem powerless are always taking some steps to respond, even if those steps are not noticed by others, or not able to stop the oppression (Wade, 1997; M. White, 2004a; Yuen, 2007). Being aware of Elle's passion for feminism, and her love for her mother, I gently proposed wondering together about how to make sense of Joy "not standing up" to Elle's brother. Elle thought this might be interesting, so we began to examine the story of family violence through a feminist lens.

We considered the time period of the 1950s when Elle's parents had married, and the 1960s to 1980s when they were raising their children. We considered cultural understandings about the role of the mother; the psychiatric history of mother-blame for children's "bad behaviour" and any "emotional problems"; understandings about family violence, including women being blamed for the occurrence of violence by men and boys, and the assumption that it was the woman's role to stop violence; and the idea that family issues need to "stay behind closed doors". We noted that these messages about women and about gender roles are shaped by patriarchy. This led to questions about isolation and support. Would Joy have been likely to speak with friends about her son's use of violence? Would she have considered turning to others in her community or to professional services or other authorities? How might others at that time have responded to a mother trying to speak up about her son hitting her and his sister? Would police intervention have been likely to be helpful, or to have made things worse?[21] Elle noticed that as well as being unsupported and isolated by the constraints of patriarchy, her mother was also physically isolated because the family had moved to the Northern Beaches of Sydney. This area was notorious for being cut off from other parts of Sydney due to distance and a lack of public transport. Elle's mother did not have a driver's licence – again perhaps a feature of the time period and patriarchal expectations about gender roles. This meant her mother was away from extended family and from friends. If she had contemplated breaking the rules about keeping family issues behind closed doors, she had little opportunity to act on it. We also wondered about the size and physical strength of her brother as he got older, and the potential that, as well as being afraid of him, Elle's mother may not have been physically able to restrain him.

I was also curious about why Elle's father was missing from the story, knowing that her parents were married. Why was Elle's sense of "not being protected" focused on her mother? Did she have a sense of expectation that her father would intervene in any way? Elle thought this was a good question! She knew her father as a loving and gentle man who would not have modelled violence, but she was unclear about how he had responded to the situation. She did recall that he was often away for work reasons.

---

21 Caulfield (2021) discussed the ways that police interventions in situations of family violence often replicate and reinforce the power and control dynamics of family violence.

Even today, social workers and therapists are still working towards making fathers more visible in their responses to family concerns, and in allocating responsibility with the person using violence against their family. Why do men seem to be invisible when it comes to addressing family issues, and violence in particular? What dominant ideas of masculinity might her brother have been influenced by at school or among his peers? Was her brother seen as being responsible for his use of violence?

We wondered what it was like for Elle's mother to try to respond to these acts of violence and to try to make sense of what was happening to their family without support and likely with a sense of self-blame. What was it like to watch her husband leave for his dream job in the city, or interstate, while she wrestled with these concerns at home?

We thought about the timeline of feminism, and that despite the emergence of second-wave feminism in Australia in the 1960s and 70s, it was a difficult time of struggling to change old views and institutions. Coming from a conservative white middle-class family and holding traditional Christian beliefs, Elle's mother may not have been able to easily step outside of traditional role expectations.[22] In deconstructing the historical period and the physical location, Elle was able to recall another cultural consideration: the bohemian scene in Sydney that was challenging traditional ideas about marriage and monogamy. Elle's father had been part of this scene, but because of her beliefs and her isolation in their home on the Northern Beaches, her mother was not connected to the scene. Elle and I wondered what effect this had on the relationship between her parents. What was it like for one partner to be holding to traditional roles and ideas, and the other to be exploring an alternative subculture? Elle guessed that there had been a renegotiation of the marriage over time, and that it was not what either of them had expected when they first became engaged.

---

[22] The documentary *Brazen Hussies* (Dwyer, Foxworthy, & Campey, 2020) described how counter-cultural feminism was in the 1960s and 70s and the huge amount of resistance feminists encountered from society at large, including both the conversative right and men on the left, such as those in the trade union movement. The key to bringing change was solidarity and accountability among women, and this was achieved through consciousness-raising groups in which women could examine challenging situations and discuss or role play how to respond (hooks, 2014; C. White, 2016a). In thinking back on my conversation with Elle, it becomes even more evident that the isolation Elle's mother faced put her in the very difficult position of trying to respond to family violence on her own.

Elle: When I think about all we've talked about today, and think about my mum's life from that perspective, there is a feeling of her being trapped, suffocated. I was angry before that she didn't protect me, but now I feel bad for her.

Loretta: When you say you feel bad for her, what would you be wishing for her if things could have been different?

Elle: An acknowledgment – for her to be seen for who she was; to be respected; to be equal.

This re-engagement with history from a feminist perspective allowed a new understanding to emerge, and this revealed absent-but-implicit (M. White, 2000b) values and hopes: a longing for Elle's mother to "be seen for who she was; to be respected; to be equal". I was so moved by this retelling.

Interestingly, as the dominant understanding was unsettled, it made space for other stories to emerge from the shadows of memory.

Elle: There was never any pressure from Mum for me to be different to how I was. Her attitude was a different attitude to that of her sister, my aunty, who always made me feel like I wasn't the way a girl "should" be – nice, neat, contained, pretty.

This had us wondering how her mother had been able to step away from traditional ideas of how a girl should present herself, even though it may be assumed that Elle's mother was brought up with dominant ideas of femininity, as suggested by her sister's opinions.

Returning to the story of violence, but this time thinking about steps her mother did take, another story emerged.

Elle: Mum eventually asked my brother to leave when he was an older teen in order to end the violence.

Loretta: What did that mean for you, in terms of your day-to-day experience of life, or your relationship with your mum?

Elle: She had time and energy then to take me to dance classes.
             I remember a warmth in our relationship. We would sing
             together. This was fun and really special. I remember at this time
             there was a sense of us being a team.

I was so delighted to hear these stories and to witness a fuller picture of Elle's
mother and of their relationship. Elle seemed delighted too, and in the next
session she spoke about how meaningful this had been to her.

Considerations of power: Looking at history through the lens of the #MeToo movement

Elle shared a story with me that she had previously not told anyone. In our
previous session, we had been re-examining a story of her mother through
a feminist lens, noticing what her mother had been up against in the family
and in the social and political context. Towards the end of this conversation,
Elle had let me know there was something she wanted to speak about next
time – something she had been thinking about in light of the #MeToo
movement.[23]

Elle wondered whether this story too could be re-examined, as it had
shaped the way she saw herself. When Elle was younger, she had been a stage
actor. After hearing stories in the media from other young women actors, she
had recently realised she had been quite powerless in a situation many years
ago, and it had her wondering whether the choices she had made had really
been "choices". Elle also spoke of a recent Australian podcast series focused
on investigating the 1982 disappearance of a woman, Lynette Dawson, who
was presumed (by the investigative journalist who produced the podcast,
Hedley Thomas [2018a], and many others) to have been murdered by her
husband. Lynette's husband, Chris Dawson, was a teacher at a local high
school. During the investigation, Thomas had inadvertently uncovered

---

[23] The term "Me Too" was first used in this context by Tarana Burke (2021) who founded
an organisation in USA to support the wellbeing of women of colour and to respond to
the issue of sexual violence. It gained widespread use after actor Alyssa Milano used it as
a hashtag on Twitter in 2017 to encourage women to speak out about sexual abuse in the
film industry.

a culture of male high-school teachers during the 1980s in the Northern Beaches area of Sydney having "relationships" with 15- and 16-year-old female students (Thomas, 2018a, 2018b). I have since listened to this podcast series, and witnesses have alleged that this was a well-known secret at the time within the school system and community. Elle had grown up in this part of Sydney and told me it was considered "quite normal" for young teens to be in relationships with men in their 20s and 30s.[24]

Knowing that these stories were in the background of Elle's decision to speak with me, I entered the next session with the sense that what we were going to be speaking about was connected with power. Knowing that Elle had never told anyone before, I wanted to ensure I created a safe space. I was aware that I was responsible for the way I listened, the questions I asked and for addressing my own power as a therapist (M. White, 1995b). I felt privileged that Elle had chosen to speak with me, and I wondered how to make visible the forces that had kept her silenced.

Elle had said that events from 30 years ago had shaped the way she saw herself in the present. White (1995a) suggested that it is the meaning that a person makes from an event that affects their sense of self, rather than the event itself. This focused me on hearing what meaning Elle had made from these, as yet unspoken, events. Holding a critical constructivist perspective (M. White, 1992), we assume that meaning-making is not done in isolation. I was keen to explore who or what had recruited Elle into these beliefs (M. White, 1992) and how they had done this.

Elle told me about travelling to the UK after high school to study acting and landing her first job in a theatre production. She described how the director seemed very scary, storming about the stage and yelling at people. This felt intimidating to Elle, but as the youngest and least experienced member of the cast, she felt invisible and seemed to have escaped his direct attention. Out of the blue, he invited her to lunch. She didn't know why the director had invited her. When I asked her what she had guessed at that time, she said she had suspected that he wasn't happy with her acting, and

---

[24] The Teacher's Pet podcast reported that claims were made by students involving approximately 20 teachers from three different schools in the area. The NSW Police subsequently commenced investigations into the allegations, and some students chose to take legal action (Maunder, 2019). In 2022, Chris Dawson, the husband of Lynette Dawson, was found guilty of her murder ("Chris Dawson", 2019; Parkes-Hupton, 2022).

that she might be fired from her job. During this lunch in a restaurant, he had touched her sexually under the table, out of view of the other patrons. Elle told me she was very shocked and didn't know what to do. Even though Elle articulated this as an unwanted and shocking moment, in the telling of it, self-blame emerged: "Why didn't I react? I just froze." "How could I have not known this would happen? I was used to predatory men. Why didn't I see this coming? This really took me by surprise."

I asked some questions to get a clearer picture of the sequence of events and some deconstruction questions to make the power relations more visible.

> To assist people to establish an account of the politics of their experience helps to undermine the self-blame and the shame that is so often experienced in relation to the blame itself. (M. White, 1995a, p. 88)

In asking more about what she had been subjected to, I was careful not to ask for further details about the assault itself but more about the context, as I did not want to retraumatise Elle (M. White, 2004a; Yuen, 2007). I was also interested to hear about ways she did respond (Wade, 1997; M. White, 2004a; Yuen, 2007):

- You said that you should have reacted, but you just froze.
  Have you heard of other people freezing when being touched unexpectedly in this way?

- What do you know now about freezing that perhaps wasn't known 30 years ago?

Elle confirmed that she now knows about "freezing" as a response to threat, but in the past people just spoke about "fight or flight" and she hadn't felt that she had done either of those things. Despite now being familiar with the concept of freezing as a protective action, there were thoughts or voices that were telling Elle that she should have done something more. The questions below were shaped by Elle's answers.

- What does this "I should have" voice tell you that you should have done?

- So it tells you that you should have walked out or yelled at him. What was it about this particular situation that made it more difficult to yell at him?

- Given the social pressure to be quiet in a restaurant and the English/ Australian cultural idea of "not making a scene", do you think this contributed to you not yelling?

- Do you think he deliberately chose a restaurant so that it would be harder to respond loudly?

- You said this was your first job, and that you were the youngest and least experienced in the cast. Given that the #MeToo movement has been in your thoughts lately, what are you thinking now about your own vulnerability?

- Did this vulnerability and the worry you felt about losing your job influence you in not walking out? Was this a small influence, a big influence or no influence?

- This director was much older than you and was respected in the theatre community. You were the newest and youngest among the actors. Do you think it was strategic that he picked the most powerless member of the cast?

- Even though you couldn't yell or walk out, were there other ways you were responding? Perhaps things you were thinking to yourself?

As this conversation progressed and we re-examined and challenged the idea that Elle had done nothing to respond to the actions of the director, Elle told me that these ideas had convinced her that she "didn't have boundaries with men" and that she "couldn't be honest in relationships". This had a lasting effect on her sense of herself over the next 30 years. In asking her where these ideas came from, it came to light that after the first time in the restaurant, the director had continued to corner her, imposing himself on her in dark corridors and other places backstage during rehearsals. However, he always made it seem that it was consensual. I have heard from other women who have been subjected to sexual assault that they are often convinced by the perpetrators that they are somehow complicit, bringing a sense of shame. In Elle's situation, the director made it appear that this was an affair, often saying "This is an awful thing that you are doing to your boyfriend", which made her feel like "a bad person". In wanting to address this, I offered an editorial of the conversation up to this point (M. White, 2007):

Loretta: You've been calling this an affair, but you said this was reflecting what the director was calling it. The way you described your sense of powerlessness, your reluctance, your fear about losing your job, his persistence, and the way each encounter seemed like a "surprise attack", it sounds to me like a series of assaults. What do you think? What would you call it?

Elle: Yes, it does seem like sexual assault – a series of assaults.

Elle mentioned an article by Ronan Farrow (2017) about the alleged tactics of producer Harvey Weinstein[25] and the effects of this on the women he sexually assaulted. Many of them spoke about a sense of guilt at not having been able to fight him off or run away, and some said that they eventually "gave up". One woman said she "feigned enjoyment, because she thought it was the only way the assault would end" (Farrow, 2017). Another woman, who disclosed in the article that he "forced himself on me sexually", described needing to continue seeing Weinstein in a professional capacity and that it may have seemed like their interactions were unaffected, despite her experience of "horror, disbelief and shame" (Farrow, 2017). She felt that she would not be able to win a legal case against him if she reported it to police because of his access to a large and experienced legal team, and she feared he would ruin her reputation in the industry. She said, "I was in

---

[25] My conversations with Elle took place in 2018. In 2020, Weinstein was convicted in New York of a criminal sex act in the first degree and of rape in the third degree (Pilkington, 2020). He was later convicted in Los Angeles of rape and other sexual offences (Dalton, 2022).

a vulnerable position, and I needed my job … It just increases the shame and guilt" (Farrow, 2017). Other women who were able to evade his attacks said their careers had been affected. Discussing this article and other stories in the media was useful in considering with Elle what makes it hard for women to speak up about workplace sexual assault or harassment. We also found it useful to hear these other women's stories as we considered how and why Elle had been able to maintain working within the theatre company during the season, despite the theatre director's ongoing sexual attacks on her, which he called "an affair".

We also spent time looking at the idea that "I should have known what would happen. I was used to predatory men". When I asked about this, Elle told me that when she was a young teenager, she had been in relationships with older men in their 20s and 30s. At the time she was not aware of the power differences, but said that looking back it became obvious. She wished she had been advised or protected by her family, but given the culture of the Northern Beaches of Sydney in the 1970s, no-one suggested that the men's age, gender, sexual experience, money, and therefore, power were an issue. Connecting this context with what happened later with the director, Elle said, "These earlier relationships had me used to being invaded". Elle realised that these men had approached her with compliments, and if the director had done this, perhaps she would have seen it as a warning sign. She was terrified of the director and his volatile rage. He never gave her compliments. She had thought she was invisible to him, so didn't suspect that he was going to target her. We wondered if yelling and raging around the stage yet ignoring her up until inviting her to lunch had been a tactic. We wondered whether instead of using compliments as a form of grooming (which would have put Elle on guard), perhaps making her more frightened about losing her job could possibly have been a tactic to make it harder for Elle to speak out. Elle stated that there was no way of knowing, but it was certainly interesting to consider.

Elle had raised this situation in the context of thinking about other actors and the #MeToo movement's allegations of abusive and predatory actions by powerful people in the industry, like Harvey Weinstein. Despite this context, the thought that emerged during our conversation that it wasn't "an affair" was described by Elle as "revolutionary". In response to a question about what effect this revolutionary thought had, Elle said she felt angry at him and at the way this had affected her life for so many years. She felt compassion for her younger self: "it was a difficult situation she was in."

Carefully enquiring about the effects of our conversation

In the next session, I was careful to ensure that I asked Elle about the effects of our previous conversation. There were several reasons for this. First, I wanted to check whether she had felt safe during our conversation, or whether there was something else I needed to do to support Elle to feel safe in our conversations. The second purpose was to check whether any negative voices had tried to attack her after breaking this long silence. I am aware that silencing by people who abuse is backed up by many dominant discourses, and that after leaving the counselling room, those dominant discourses can create thoughts that attack people who have broken the rules of silence. Third, if I didn't mention such a significant conversation, it could potentially be interpreted by Elle as me not feeling comfortable with our conversation, further adding to the silencing. Fourth, in focusing on the difference in power to explore the dynamics of abuse, I was concerned that I may have contributed to a sense of powerlessness for Elle because we hadn't given enough space to exploring her responses or acts of resistance to the abuse. We had explored responses to some degree, but Elle found these questions more difficult. Lastly, I wondered whether any new revolutionary thoughts had occurred in between our meetings.

In enquiring about this previous conversation, and what had made it possible to speak, Elle said, "That door had been shut. The #MeToo movement was a way in". This had us acknowledging the contributions of other women who had spoken out, and Elle named particular women whose testimonies had influenced her. She also said she had felt safe in our conversations, and that previous sessions had made it possible for us to build a relationship of trust before entering into this difficult topic. Elle identified that an important part of building safety had been that in the earlier sessions we had explored her values and the influences on these values. She said that this made her "feel seen as a person and not just as a person with problems". In narrative therapy terms, we might think of this as getting to know the person outside of the problem and also helping build a safe "territory of identity" (M. White, 2005) before embarking on more difficult conversations. Elle expressed that this differed from other experiences of therapy. Elle's reflections on the process are further detailed below as we did some co-research about this after completing our work together.

In terms of thoughts that had occurred to Elle in between sessions, she said that she had been questioning why she hadn't spoken to her boyfriend at the time, who was caring and who could have supported her to take legal action if she'd wanted to pursue that. During the week, Elle had realised that she "didn't have a concept at that time of being able to ask for protection from him. I think this was a legacy of not feeling protected as a child".

Elle was now in a committed and loving lesbian relationship. Flow-on effects of our conversation had been that Elle had been able to speak to her partner about these assaults, and that her partner's response had been very protective and caring. This provided another witnessing of Elle's suffering and an acknowledgment of the effects of this suffering. Her partner's caring response was very meaningful to Elle.

During the week, Elle had been angry at the director. She felt that he had been intentional in positioning her as "complicit and silent". I was thinking about the anger and wondering which values, beliefs or principles were absent but implicit in this (M. White, 2000b). I was also thinking that this idea of "complicity" and its meaning to Elle needed further exploration. There had been some negative thoughts or attacks on Elle since breaking her silence. She said, "I feel stupid. There is a group of voices saying, 'You were 23. Perfectly capable of making a decision'".

At this point in our conversation, Elle's demeanour completely changed. She seemed to shrink, and her head lowered. This alerted me to the possibility that this group of voices was having an influence, that shame could have entered the room, or that trauma was affecting her. I try to be alert to such body signals and to attend to them immediately, otherwise the rest of the conversation can be derailed by shame or self-blame. It might be a problem we have already explored, or it might be a friend or cousin of the problem. This practice of stopping immediately when noticing changes in the body or demeanour of the person, and externalising the problem or exposing the thoughts, was introduced to me by Marilyn O'Neill years ago in supervision. I have found it a very useful practice.

Loretta: Elle, I noticed that you slumped down just now, and you've gone quiet. I'm wondering what thought or feeling popped in a moment ago.

Elle: I feel really ashamed.

Loretta: Oh dear, I've noticed this has happened to others when speaking about abuse – that Shame[26] seems to walk on into the room. Is it okay if we spend a few minutes noticing this Shame and finding out its intentions?

Elle: Okay.

Loretta: This might seem like a weird question, but if you could visualise Shame, what would it look like? Does it have a shape or colour?

Elle: It's brown, wet, solid and thick.

Loretta: Where in the room is it right now?

Elle: It's covering me.

Loretta: What is it saying?

Elle: Shame is saying, "This is all about me. You might not be able to have a conversation without me".

Loretta: Does that mean that Shame is wanting to be present in our conversation or to stop us from having a conversation?

Elle: Shame thinks it's the main player. It wants to keep a lid on things.

Loretta: Are you okay with it covering you and trying to keep a lid on things, or would you prefer we move it to another place so we can have our conversation?

---

[26] Here I have capitalised the word "Shame" to emphasise the externalisation and characterisation of shame as a force in Elle's life

Elle decided to move it away from her and have it sit in the corner of the room, facing towards the window.

Loretta: Now that we have moved it to the corner, what tactics are you able to notice that it has been using against you? Or what weapons does it have?

Elle: It has me believe that I am powerless and not worthy. I'm not a good person.

Loretta: What is meant by "a good person"? How would this be defined and by whom? How has Shame convinced you that you are not a good person? Has someone supported this idea?

Elle traced this back to her early teen years when her brother colluded with Shame, trying to tell her things about herself. As she entered into relationships, he told her she was "promiscuous", despite he himself having many sexual relationships. This had her thinking she was not a good person. We then spent some time deconstructing gendered discourses about sex in Western society and their links with shame around female sexuality. Elle noticed that when these discourses are utilised, Shame makes it hard for young women to speak with parents or trusted older women about their sexual relationships. Elle considered that it may have been really useful, as a teen, to speak to an adult about her relationships with older men.

Loretta: Who benefits when women are silenced by Shame?

Elle: Sleezy men.

Loretta: As we have been speaking about Shame and its tactics and support network, 1 have noticed that you've begun sitting up straighter, and your voice seems more confident. Can I just check with you where Shame is now, and what is happening to it? Is it still looking the same?

Elle: It is becoming translucent. It's melting like a snowman.

Loretta: How do you account for this change? Why is it melting?

Elle: Seeing how Shame serves men in these situations – in my situation and for other women I know.

Loretta: What has this got you thinking about now?

Elle: I'm thinking about your earlier question, "What is a good person?" Telling someone they are not a good person is a really powerful strategy to silence women. It gets them thinking they are not worthy. My brother did it and the director did it. I can see now how manipulative this is.

Predicting and preparing for comebacks of the problem

While working with people in relation to a range of problems, I have discovered that even after a conversation that seems to have separated the person from the problem, the problem can make a comeback. This can happen for a variety of reasons, such as: the strength and pervasiveness of dominant discourses in society; returning to a family environment where the problem is quite active or has a strong hold; or a long history of repetitive negative thoughts and beliefs leading to a well-worn track of thinking (Beaudoin, 2019).

Predicting a comeback and preparing for this can be useful, not to bring fear to the person, but to ensure that if a problem does try to get its hooks back in, they will be on guard for early warning signs. This can have them taking some steps early on to address the comeback. David Newman told me about the concept of predicting comebacks, and I have found it really useful. If the problem really makes a strong attack, I have noticed that having predicted this can reduce a sense of failure, especially in relation to problems like self-harm, troubles with eating, or problematic alcohol or drug use.

I asked Elle, "As we finish our conversation and you head back into your week, how might you keep separated from Shame? I'm just wondering if it might try to stage a comeback. What do you think?"

Elle agreed that Shame might try to influence her again, but she described some ways she would keep separated from it. This included drawing on her knowledge of poststructuralist theories and our conversation deconstructing

Shame: having recognised that Shame is constructed, it could then be deconstructed. Elle also thought that her Buddhist practices would support her. When she noticed the voice of Shame, she could take a moment to bring her attention to her body and "come into the present moment". Then she could "allow the storyline to dissolve and just sit gently with the sensations". Elle said this method helped when she had intrusive thoughts. Elle could also identify three beliefs that would be useful: "there is nothing in this situation to feel shame about"; "even the self is an illusion"; "we are interdependent with others".

Two weeks later, Elle returned to speak with me. After discussing some current concerns, we spoke about the ongoing reflections Elle was having about our previous two conversations. Elle filled me in a bit more about the Teacher's Pet podcast she had been listening to (Thomas, 2018a). It was revealing a lot to Elle about the context she had grown up in. Elle shared the investigative journalist's incredulity that no-one had pursued concerns that a woman was missing. Friends and family were worried, but as Lynette Dawson's disappearance had been reported to police by her husband, they assumed that it was being followed up. However, the police believed the husband's story that she had "run off", possibly visiting friends or possibly joining a cult. This had Elle thinking about the way women (particularly "housewives") are not valued in society, and the way the police have often failed to take crimes against women seriously.[27] The main issue Elle wanted to explain to me from the podcast was that at the time Lynette went missing, Lynette's husband had been having a sexual relationship with one of his high-school students. The podcast reported that many teachers at this high school and other high schools in the area were having sexual relationships with their female students who were 15 and 16 years old. I have since listened to this podcast, and in the episode titled "Hopeless", the journalist says the attitude at the time had been described to him as teachers seeing sex with students as "classroom fringe benefits" (Thomas, 2018b).

---

[27] At the time of our conversations, Chris Dawson had not been arrested by police. The podcast brought widespread attention to the case, and he has since been arrested, tried and convicted of Lynette Dawson's murder ("Chris Dawson", 2019; Parkes-Hupton, 2022).

Loretta: What impact does hearing about this have on you?

Elle: It helps me understand the culture I grew up in. People didn't
            question it. Men had sex with underage girls.

We also discussed newspaper reports that Elle had found revealing about
what was going on for other teens in her social network, aspects of culture
during that time period that may have influenced Elle and her family.

Elle: My life makes more sense. Thinking about this culture counteracts
            the Shame we've spoken about. I can understand the passivity
            that was part of my relationships with older men. My family
            never questioned these relationships. I see things differently now
            and wonder about the issues of power.

Loretta: Thinking about the context, and about your current
            understandings of power, seems to be counteracting Shame.
            When Shame is counteracted, what else is possible?

Elle: I feel compassion for myself.

Loretta: We have to finish our conversation in a few minutes, but
            I am just wondering, if this compassion kept building, what is
            your guess about what you would be noticing? What might it
            make space for? What might be different this coming week or
            month?

Elle: I would be visited by Shame less. It would make space for
            something like confidence. An ease might grow.

Three months later

Elle returned from a trip to the UK and told me she had visited the area where
she had lived and worked during her time in the theatre. Elle noticed that
reflecting on the past through our conversations had allowed her to bring
a new perspective as she'd wandered the familiar streets. She had developed

a greater understanding, which allowed a sense of tenderness towards her younger self. She also felt less confused about that period of her life.

Loretta: What did you understand differently now?

Elle: What the director did affected me. I changed. I broke up with my boyfriend because I had lost faith in myself. There is complexity in sexual transgressions – I hadn't thought of it as abuse because complicity seemed to equal responsibility. I made assumptions about myself, that I couldn't be trusted, so I withdrew.

Loretta: Has that been important to think about?

Elle: Yes, because I never really understood what happened: why something that was good – my relationship with my boyfriend – ended. Now I can look at myself with tenderness and look at the relationship with him with tenderness.

Loretta: What did that tenderness make possible for you as you were walking through the streets?

Elle: It helps me understand myself and process the confusion. I can say to my younger self, "You can ask for help". It makes me think that instead of being shrouded in guilt, she could have asked her boyfriend for help. It's possible that he would have had an understanding of the power dynamic that she didn't have, due to his own study and his work. She was so passive.

Loretta: The idea of passivity has come back to haunt you again?

Elle: Yes, it seems strong.

I invited Elle to reflect on times this sense of passivity had been previously examined.

Loretta: Is there anything we have talked about that has got you thinking differently about this idea of passivity?

Elle: I see passivity as not having done anything to stop the director
            or report him after the very first time, but when we spoke about
            how he deliberately got me stoned straight after it, that made me
            see that it was hard to think straight, to see what to do. It also
            might have made me seem less credible if I had decided to go to
            the police.

Loretta: So it's been helpful to think about the director getting you stoned
            as a deliberate tactic to make it harder for you to think and harder
            to report him?

Elle: Yes.

Loretta: I'm thinking about it being the 1980s, not now in 2018, and the
            fear you had about losing your job. We hadn't had the #MeToo
            movement yet, so you didn't know what other actors were
            experiencing.

Elle: Pieces are falling into place of how I got here. Part of me is pissed
            off at the director. Part of me has a sadness for the young couple
            my boyfriend and I were – neither of us understanding why our
            relationship fell apart. If I could have told him, we could have
            done something together about the director.

Building further connections between individual and collective experience

We acknowledged again the various factors that had made it not seem to
be an option at that time to speak to anyone, including her boyfriend. We
also spoke about the gathering momentum of the #MeToo movement.
Elle described the importance for her of watching eight hours live of the
Kavanaugh hearing (a hearing to consider whether a judge, Brett Kavanaugh,
should be appointed to the US Supreme Court after allegations of sexual
assault were made [see D. Smith, 2018]). Elle experienced hearing university
professor Christine Blasey Ford's testimony about being subjected to sexual
assault by Kavanaugh as a teen and the way this testimony was received by

politicians and the wider community as "both fascinating and triggering". It was significant for Elle that someone with such strong credibility as Dr Ford had spoken out about sexual assault. Unfortunately, we saw that her testimony was treated with contempt by people who didn't want to consider that a high-profile judge could have previously behaved in this way, or who didn't want to experience the political repercussions of believing her testimony.

During the hearing, Senator Dianne Feinstein, a member of the Senate Judiciary Committee, spoke about the experiences of women speaking up about sexual assault, and why many wait many years before telling anyone (Barajas & Bush, 2018; PBS Newshour, 2018). Feinstein mentioned a conversation she had with a constituent whose life had been impacted by an attempted rape and who had not told anyone for 40 years. Often people who disclose sexual assault are questioned about why they did not speak up earlier; however, there are many barriers to disclosure. Additionally, some who did speak up at the time were not believed or were punished for speaking up.

Senator Feinstein said:

I think it is important to remember these realities as we hear from Dr Ford about her experience.

There's been a great deal of public discussion about the #MeToo movement today verses the Year of the Woman almost 27 years ago. But while young women are standing up and saying, "No more," our institutions have not progressed in how they treat women who come forward. Too often, women's memories and credibility come under assault. In essence, they are put on trial and forced to defend themselves and often re-victimized in the process. ("Kavanaugh hearing", 2018)

Elle said, "The #MeToo movement is so important – the way it is playing out, the impact of it. The people who come forward are incredibly brave to talk about it and possibly not be believed. A lot still needs to be done, but I believe the times are changing: what is acceptable and not acceptable, especially in the workplace, is changing."

White (2001), in his paper "Folk psychology and narrative practice", described the potential impact of exploring dominant and alternative storylines as opening space for a

> reflexive engagement with life ... a capacity to achieve distance in relation to the immediacy of life ... to review the events of our lives from other vantage points ... This reading of our lives through narrative structures provides the opportunity for us to render meaningful that which previously wasn't, and to re-conceive of that which has already been rendered meaningful. (M. White, 2001, p. 91)

White went on to describe how this reflexive engagement or "creative re-engagement", this "generation and re-generation of meaning [that] occurs across time" (2001, p. 92), opens up new options for the future. This is because it gets people more connected to their purposes, commitments and moral considerations, which may not have been previously articulated in relation to past or current stories, understandings and predicaments. This new understanding of why events turned out the way they did, and what this might mean for the future, lights up new opportunities for action and new ways to address predicaments, contributing to a stronger sense of agency.

In my work with Elle, I witnessed this regeneration of meaning in relation to her understanding of her mother. A richer, multi-storied and more nuanced understanding then opened up new appreciations, not just of her mother and their shared past, but also their current relationship. I also witnessed this in relation to Elle's understanding of her response to the workplace sexual assaults, which offered a more compassionate view of herself. Our conversations, and then Elle's trip back overseas, opened up a revision of her understanding of why the relationship with her boyfriend had ended. Elle also revised her understanding of the relationships she'd had as a teenager with older men, and how she had previously been shamed for this by her brother. By looking through a feminist lens at culture and power, and hearing the stories of other young people through the Teacher's Pet podcast (Thomas, 2018a) and other reports, Elle came to understand that there had been a culture of older men taking advantage of teenage girls, and that the community had stood by silently. This reduced the shame Elle felt, and opened up space for other emotions such as indignation. These new understandings then connected with Elle's values, hopes and intentions through re-authoring practices and exploration of the absent but implicit (M. White, 2000b), which in turn created a preferred sense of self and a richer array of life options moving forward.

In the years since meeting with Elle, I have continued to hear many other stories from women about sexual harassment and sexual assault in the workplace. As already discussed, there are many reasons that women may find it hard to speak up about sexual harassment or assault in the workplace. Migrant women have informed me about additional barriers, such as being in small businesses, like take-away food shops or small grocery stores, in which the person who was harassing or assaulting them was a family friend or relative; or where there was no-one else on duty to discuss the behaviour with or to report to; where there was no human resources section or policy and procedures manual; or where the job was "cash in hand", making the person feel reluctant to report the assault. Women who have a family or community connection to the person who is assaulting them have told me that there are multiple concerns: that they will not be believed by their community if they speak up; or that they will be blamed for causing distress to the man's wife or children if his reputation is "tainted"; or that they will be viewed as having seduced the man and bring shame on their own family and be ostracised; or that they will not be hired by anyone else and will be in financial difficulty. For migrants who are not confident in speaking the dominant language, they may not have job opportunities outside of their own community. These factors compound their concerns about speaking up.

****

The meanings that a person makes about an event can affect the way they see themselves and the ways they move forward in life. People always find ways to respond to abuse and trauma, but these responses are not always noticed or acknowledged, even by the person themselves. When memories about responses are not available, meaning-making can reinforce feelings of shame, guilt or powerlessness. For Elle, the meanings she had made of events that had taken place 30 years ago had shaped the way she saw herself and moved through life. Reconsidering these events through a feminist lens, and in their temporal and cultural contexts, enabled Elle to develop new understandings of her own experiences, and to see others' actions in a new light. As the power relations that had informed Elle's previous meaning-making became clear, her new understandings allowed a greater appreciation for what her younger self had been up against, and this opened up fresh possibilities for moving forward in preferred ways.

This chapter also touched on the use of podcasts, news reports and current affairs in therapeutic conversations, which is a practice I have been experimenting with over several years. This theme of drawing on aspects of popular culture to scaffold conversations is taken up again in Chapter 8. Before I return to that theme, the following chapter introduces some considerations that can help to ensure that our conversations are not retraumatising for the person, even when the topic is a traumatic experience.

Reflection

- There have been various themes and practices raised in this chapter. Which aspect of the work or of Elle's story did you connect with the most?

- What was it about this that resonated for you or challenged you in some way?

- What has this got you thinking about? Is there an idea or practice you might take into your own practice?

7.
Co-researching the effects of therapeutic conversations: Addressing power and avoiding retraumatisation

Throughout this book I have shared many examples of practice in which people have spoken with me about traumatic events and relationships where there were ongoing acts of physical, emotional and/or sexual violence. This chapter includes a discussion of how we might support people when they share these difficult stories.

In "Naming abuse and breaking from its effects", Michael White (1995a) was very clear that we should not "return to the site of trauma" (1995a, p. 85) and have people simply repeat the story while viewing it through their familiar lens. Often this existing lens has the person focusing on self-blame, a sense of worthlessness or self-hate. Sometimes this view has been shaped by the person who enacted the abuse as a way to shame the person into silence. White described practices that assist people to find safer ways to explore a history of abuse. By asking people to look at themselves and the events they have experienced from a different vantage point, as I did in my work with Elle in the previous chapter, the stories of abuse can be viewed in ways that move people to express, for example, a sense of outrage over the injustice that has occurred, or an appreciation of themselves as having skills of survival, rather than compounding a negative view of themselves. This different vantage point is sometimes referred to as "the riverbank position"

(Caleb Wakhungu; as cited in Denborough, 2014, p. 22), in which a person metaphorically steps out of the river of despair, overwhelm, crisis or chaos and looks at the situation from a safe place. One way to create this safe place is to start conversations by getting to know the person outside of the problem, such as asking about their interests or passions, which leads to unearthing skills, knowledges and values.

This way of working leads to a reduced risk of retraumatisation, but people may still experience distress during a therapeutic conversation. White emphasised the need to actively encourage people to monitor their experience of a conversation.

> Throughout the process of therapy, we need to be continually consulting people about what they perceive to be the effects of our work with them, about how the reinterpretation and expression of their experience is affecting the shape of their lives, and about what they understand to be the limitations and possibilities associated with our conversations. (M. White, 1995a, p. 87)

As well as being alert to changes in posture, facial expression or tone of voice, as mentioned earlier in Elle's story, we can specifically ask people what happens for them when the thoughts or memories start to interfere, such as becoming fidgety or agitated or numb. We can ask about their skills and knowledge about what they can do when this occurs. It is useful to do this in the early stages of conversations about difficult topics. People may identify homegrown skills such as "taking a break" or "reminding myself I am safe", or they may draw on learnt skills from previous counselling or mental health groups, possibly known to them as "grounding techniques" like "taking deep breaths" or "feeling your body in the chair and your feet on the ground". If a person is struggling to identify what they do to feel calmer or safer, we might tentatively offer one of these techniques by saying something like "someone else I met with last week said that they find it useful to pause and have a glass of water, and another person said they have a breathing technique they learnt in a group. Have you tried anything like that? Has it been useful or not useful? Or would you like me to suggest something else we can try?"

We can invite people to let us know if they notice they are heading towards an unsafe feeling or if a question is not okay for them. Due to the difference in power between a person attending counselling and the counsellor, it can be useful to spend time at the beginning of the conversation asking how they will let us know if the question is not okay, or if the timing is not right (Richardson & Reynolds, 2014). We can invite them to practise, by showing us whether they would raise a hand, or shake their head, or say "I don't want to answer that today".

I have been told by some people that they prepare for a session they expect will be difficult by wearing something special, such as their favourite jumper, so they can feel safe and can touch the soft material if they feel uncomfortable during the conversation. One person, Kai, who experienced racing thoughts, wore frayed jeans so they could play with the threads to help them concentrate. We also experimented with having therapeutic putty available to play with while talking, and Kai said that during this conversation they experienced their "best concentration ever!"

Transitioning to home

In thinking about these conversations, I need to mention that I believe it is important to assist people to transition as we approach the time for leaving the session. One way was demonstrated in the transcript with Elle in the previous chapter: alerting the person that the session will be finishing in a few minutes. This can be followed by an editorial about what has been discussed and a question about what the person would like to take with them from the conversation. We may also ask if there is anything they would like to leave here. This gives the person space to reflect on the conversation, and to think about anything they might hold on to, write down or reflect further on. In asking if there is anything they may want to leave here, we can explore the positioning of counselling as a safe space for keeping certain conversations contained. These enquiries can also create space for feedback about any questions that were not okay, or that led to unhelpful avenues of enquiry.

After a conversation in which traumatic events have been discussed, we can assist the person to prepare for re-entering the outside world and their home life. I believe that it is a therapist's ethical responsibility to keep an eye on the time during a session so that we can ensure there is enough time left to end the session well. I usually ask people a few (not all) of these questions:

- We have been talking about some big things today.
  What are you planning to do after you leave here?
  Are you going to stop for a coffee or go for a walk
  and reflect on our conversation or head straight home?

- Or would you prefer to *not* reflect on our conversation.
  Might you have a coffee or go for a walk to prepare your mind
  for thinking about something else? What do you imagine,
  or know from previous experience, might be helpful?

- How will you be getting home? Are you driving or catching
  public transport?

- Will you listen to music? If so, which songs or type of music
  will you probably listen to?

- Or do you think silence is more useful for you today? I'm sure you
  know whether music or silence will be more useful for you.

- Are you meeting up with anyone after this?
  If so, who are you meeting with?

- Was planning to meet with this person after our conversation
  intended as a way of looking after yourself or not?

- What might you do when you get home?

- If our conversation raises some difficult thoughts or memories
  for you outside of this counselling space, what might you do
  with those thoughts or memories?

- If things become difficult, who might you talk to?

- What other ways do you have to look after yourself?

We can then check in at the next conversation about the effects of the last conversation. This active discussion of the effects of therapy can be seen as co-research, which seeks to create new knowledge and address the power dynamic of positioning the therapist as expert, instead repositioning the client and therapist as a collaborative team working together to respond to the problem.

Co-research

David Epston (1999) wrote about the genesis of his use of the term "co-research" in narrative practice. Although this term is also used in other contexts, Epston discussed how it is used in narrative therapy, in which therapists engage in the co-production of knowledge with persons, families or communities. One form of co-research is to have externalising conversations about the problem, finding out about its tactics, intentions, effects and so on, as well as about the ways the person/family and those in their network have responded to this type of problem. This knowledge may be documented and shared with others who are known to that person, or with others who may not be known to that person but may benefit from this knowledge, such as other people seeking assistance with a similar problem (Epston, 1999). Over the years I have learnt a lot from the people I meet with about problems and ways to get through problems. This has been invaluable to my professional work.

> A second common form of co-research involves inquiry into what is helpful or not helpful in the therapeutic conversations themselves. Throughout narrative therapy consultations, questions are asked to ensure that the conversation is being experienced as relevant and helpful. Research is also conducted at the completion of therapy to evaluate the effects of particular questions and lines of inquiry (Dulwich Centre Publications, 2004, p. 32. See also Epston & M. White, 1992; Morgan, 2000).

This second form of co-research has also been a very rich learning experience. It often surprises me to hear which questions or ideas have most stood out as useful to the person consulting me. I try to then ask what was useful about it, so as not to assume. I have also learnt about what has *not* been useful, or what could be modified to be more useful. For example, in my early encounters with narrative therapy, I was drawn to the idea of writing letters to clients: to capture what we had spoken about; to acknowledge the hardships the person was facing; to highlight what we had discovered about their skills and knowledges in responding to these hardships; to offer further questions to prompt thinking between conversations; or to ask questions that I wished I had asked but didn't during a conversation (Stevens, 2010; M. White & Epston, 1990). I carefully crafted each letter, printed it, checked it with a colleague to see if it was clear or if my intent in any sentence could be misunderstood, read it again and then posted it (having previously checked whether the person was interested in receiving a letter and whether it was safe to post it to their house). With all this caretaking, I was hopeful that these letters would be useful. David Newman (2008) reminds us that it is important to check with people about the effects of a document, or of the documenting process. Feedback he has received has suggested that a short document is most appreciated. This was echoed in the feedback I received that some of my letters were too long, or contained too many questions, or that reading while struggling with depression can be hard. In my eagerness to write the "perfect" letter, I had included too much! Now, I am finding short emails and even text messages are appreciated. This also benefits my use of time. One person really valued having a few dot points about her "skills in getting through" on a small card, which we co-created in session and laminated. This meant she could read it quickly in a time of urgent need, when concentrating on a longer text would have been difficult, and she could easily keep it in her purse to be accessed wherever it was needed.

Co-researching therapeutic conversations

During my conversations with Elle, whose story was shared in the previous chapter, I regularly checked with her about how she was going with the conversation, and whether we were on track. I also asked her about the effects of my questions. We had 10 sessions together, and during our last session we reviewed the notes from the previous sessions. I asked Elle if she wanted to look at the notes, but she said that might be overwhelming and she would prefer for me to look through them and read out some points. The notes were in the form of quotes from Elle in response to my questions. I also had made notes after some sessions about the questions I had asked, because I was curious about the direction the conversations had taken and how we had got there. As I read out some quotes from the notes, we grouped these into themes.

Elle was surprised by how much we had covered in the previous sessions. She had forgotten some of what we had spoken about in our earlier sessions, which had been six months earlier. This made me wonder whether perhaps I could have used documentation more to capture and share with Elle what had been discussed. Elle was also curious about the process of the therapy. She said, "It is interesting how much we covered before we got to the story of the director. We talked about a lot of positive things, like spirituality, my hopes for my work, my relationships. This got me to a place of safety. I'd never shared that story before (about the director), and there is not much that I don't share. The conversations were so rich. There was more than what I expected".

I asked her what had been the most useful, and Elle stated that "the ideas about Shame were so useful. The deconstruction – What is a good person? Taking the experience and the Shame head on, thinking about it and coming to clarity. I hadn't wanted to think about it, but when we did it was so useful".

She also said she liked hearing back from the notes: "I enjoyed revisiting those stories, thinking about where our conversations had gone, like our conversations about the environment when I was growing up."

Two months later, Elle generously agreed that I could write up her story to share with others. We caught up again for a longer conversation about the effects of our conversations.

Loretta: So, two months on, what stands out to you from our conversations? Is there something you've been thinking more about, or something you are curious about? Is there anything you especially want to let me and other therapists know about?

Elle: It really interests me that the story of the director came out, and that became so important to explore further. That isn't what I came to you about. We were talking about gender, internalised homophobia and sexism, and it led to this conversation about what had happened overseas. I've been wondering how we created the environment for that to come forward. It was the right environment. This story was hidden under years of avoiding it – having packed it away.

Loretta: Well, what do you think made it the right environment?

Elle: We spoke about spirituality early on, and that surprised me. I've been to therapy before, and that hadn't ever come up or been asked about. In modern society we don't usually speak about spirituality, not even with friends or colleagues.

Loretta: Are you saying this contributed to the right environment? That it impacted our later conversations in some way?

Elle: It made me feel seen. I knew you were seeing me as a whole person – the broader parts of my life.

Loretta: I remember we also talked about the political and social environment that your mum was up against in her life. This was in the conversation where at the end you told me you wanted to talk about something else about power and the #MeToo movement next time. In my mind, I'm imagining that speaking about patriarchy and social contexts led towards this. Is that right?

Elle: That was a significant conversation, but actually I'd already decided to tell you about the director, but then we started talking about my mum and the impact of violence on her life.

Loretta: Oh! Maybe I didn't make space for you to tell me about the director at the beginning of the session.

Elle: No, it wasn't that. The whole session it had been on my mind, but I just couldn't. There was so much fear. But I did have the courage to place it there – to tell you that I had something to tell you next time. And it wasn't just fear. I found the conversation about Mum really interesting, and I wanted to follow it to see where it went, so I decided to hold on to the other story.

Loretta: You had the courage to place it there. I'm so curious about that. What did it take? Did you prepare yourself in some way?

Elle: Yes, I thought about it before we met and decided to bring it up. You asked me what I want therapists to know. I want them to know how dangerous it feels to bring something up, and that if someone raises something like this, make sure you follow up on it. I was glad you brought it up the next time. You didn't forget to remind me that I'd said I wanted to talk about it.

Loretta: You've got me thinking about what it takes to bring up something difficult, and I'm reflecting on other people who meet with me. I'm wondering about how they managed it. I'm also thinking back to my own experience of counselling, and how I emailed my counsellor to let them know I wanted to talk about something hard. Then I felt like the first step was done, and I'd made the commitment to talk about it. Was it like that for you or somehow different?

Elle: Yes, once I'd told you that we would be speaking about it next time, it was easier.

Loretta: Like you'd foreshadowed[28] it, the counsellor had been prepared? Or you had prepared yourself?

Elle: Both. Yes, it is like foreshadowing. You were now expecting the story and I was ready to tell it.

---

[28] Foreshadowing is a term common in writing novels and screenplays. From what I knew of Elle's interests, I guessed that she would be familiar with this term. White (2007) and Denborough (2008) suggest we use metaphors local to the person or community.

Loretta: You've really got me thinking about what skills people must engage with in preparing counsellors. Counsellors may have thought about what skills the person has in preparing themselves to speak about something hard, but do you think people also work to prepare the counsellor?

Elle: Yes, I imagine so.

We also spoke about fear of speaking out and what it had taken for Elle to share her story.

Elle: Even now I have a complete terror of speaking out to any authority. I've been thinking about what it would be like if I wrote to my ex-boyfriend and told him what had happened to help him understand. But what if he wanted me to take legal action against the director or the theatre? It is too frightening.

Loretta: What makes it so frightening?

Elle: There are two parts. The first part is shame about not speaking up at the time. I still have a sense that this was going along with it somehow. I had a total lack of insight at the time about how it would affect my life, my sense of self – it was the main contributing factor in breaking up with my boyfriend, giving up acting, having so many years of unhappy relationships, losing trust in myself, losing confidence in dealing with men's sexuality, and then exploring my own sexual identity (although I'd had girlfriends before and boyfriends, it now made sense to make myself unavailable to men). There is something about taking a stand publicly that is terrifying. Being exposed, being subjected to other people's opinions. In every account that you hear, the person who has been assaulted, the person with less power, is totally discredited. Men deny. This hasn't changed, we've seen it recently in the news. Women are discredited.

Loretta: So the way society responds and what you have witnessed of that?

Elle: Yes. Another thing apart from the media is the legal system. When I was an acting student at 16 years of age, I was part of a student film project that was an improvisation. My role was as a rape victim appearing in court. I had to be on the stand. I remember it as the experience of being ripped apart – of the way words can do that and that the system supports that. It made me frightened of ever going to court.

The second part that is frightening about speaking out about what happened to me is the idea of severity – the severity of a violent assault as compared to one where the issue is about power and consent. Power and consent have been blurry issues, but #MeToo is making space for these issues to be spoken about. It is not okay for men to just grab at women. With Trump's "grab 'em by the pussy" comment about women [see "Transcript", 2017], a lot of people were outraged by that, but this outrage seems kind of new.

Loretta: Yeah, and despite outrage from some, he still got elected as president of the USA. I really thought that was the end for him, but people seemed to accept it, or forgive him, or move on. I found that quite shocking.

Elle: Yeah, me too. What has been most shocking for me, looking back at the situation with the director, is seeing what an incredible influence this has had on my life. It totally changed the course of my life. I hadn't appreciated that before. I had kept it out of sight.

Loretta: What has looking at it made possible? What have been the effects?

Elle: I think this is still quite fresh, I'm still processing it. But it has opened up an area of healing. It has helped me understand things I never could – ending my relationship with my boyfriend, why my life took a dramatic turn that I hadn't attributed to this. Everything had been okay: where I was living, who I was living with, working as an actor abroad, my future. I threw it all away to return to Australia. Now I have compassion for myself.

Loretta: Given how frightening you've said it is to speak out, do you think telling me about this, telling your partner, telling the people who will read your story, do you think these are acts of resistance to silencing, or standing up to fear, or to Shame, or would you call these actions something else?

Elle: When I returned to the UK recently, and walked through those streets again, it gave me time to reflect. It took me back to that time. I had a strong desire to share my story – this is important for other people to know that sexual assault that isn't violent, that is by someone that you know, these types of assaults are easily dismissed as mistakes you made. But when you look at them again, you can see that these events would benefit from being examined and deconstructed. These ideas you have had of yourself for so long, stories that you have held on to for so long, can be re-examined.

Loretta: Thank you so much for sharing this with others. I imagine it will make a real difference to the lives of other women, either through reading it themselves, or through the flow-on effect of therapists having an understanding informed by your knowledge. What has this process been like for you, speaking about this again after a couple of months have passed by?

Elle: It is positive to keep processing it. Having this conversation has been another opportunity for reflection. I just want to get the message out that those things that have happened that we might have dismissed, in taking it to therapy there can be such a richness of understanding. I'm shocked at what an impact this event 30 years ago has had on my life, and how revisiting it has opened up an area of healing.

****

Elle's reflections about our previous therapeutic work were part of a process of co-research not only about her story and the skills and knowledge she had discovered, but also about the effects of our conversations.

In order to avoid talking about trauma in ways that might invite people to re-live traumatic events or that risk reinforcing negative identity conclusions, it is imperative that we invite people to join us in ensuring that our therapeutic conversations are going well and are not retraumatising. Establishing a "riverbank" position can offer a new vantage point from which the person can recognise their survival skills and the hopes they have sustained despite the effects of the trauma.

Through challenging power imbalances and avoiding the positioning of the therapist as expert, we can invite people to actively participate in ensuring that conversations are going well. That can involve establishing safe ways for people to let us know when a question or topic is not what they want to talk about right now.

For Elle, earlier conversations about "spirituality" helped to create a sense of "safety" and being seen as a "whole person". This made it feel possible to talk about her experience with the director. The theme of spirituality is taken up in Chapter 9. First, we turn to conversations about sexual assault in the workplace, and the possibilities for solidarity and collective action.

Reflection

- In what ways do you utilise co-research?

- What have you discovered?

- Have you adapted your practice according to these discoveries?

- Who would you like to honour as you reflect on your learnings in this work?

8.
Linking stories:
From individual responses
to solidarity in the workplace

The focus of this chapter is on linking stories so that people don't feel alone in their experiences, so that problems can be understood as existing in a social context, and as a basis for acting in solidarity with others. I draw on work with people who have experienced sexual assault or harassment in large companies and government departments. This includes work with Anna, who agreed to share her story about responding to workplace harassment, seeking support but not receiving it from her human resources manager, and finding connection and solidarity with others. Links can be made between individuals who may never meet or within people's networks. Links can also come through engagement with cultural resources like movies, songs and reporting of current events. This linking of stories can assist people in seeing experience as collective, social and political, not as isolated events for which they are responsible. This chapter introduces work with Anna, and also draws on the work with Elle that was the focus of Chapter 6.

Anna's story

Anna, who worked for a government agency, told me that she had changed jobs, and that one of the reasons was to escape sexual harassment. After Anna had turned down a male colleague who asked for a date, he began telling untrue stories to other colleagues about sexual encounters with her.

She tried to address it with him, and to "smooth things over without him losing face". He didn't stop spreading lies about her. He actually increased the harassment, sending her verbally abusive text messages and writing negative things about her on social media, which work colleagues would see.

I asked Anna about how this had affected her, and she said his response had her feeling that "something must be wrong with me. I didn't think I gave him any signals, but he said I was leading him on. It makes me think that I should not be friendly to men at work, in case they misunderstand". Even though she had left this workplace, the effects were still lingering for Anna. We wondered together what it would mean to Anna to "be less friendly" and she thought it would be awful. It would require her to not smile at colleagues and to never ask about how they were going. It would cost Anna her value of "friendliness" and her expression of "happiness". In asking Anna to take a position on this, she stated that it was not okay that this man's sexual harassment might cost her these values. Looking at this from a feminist perspective, Anna noted that blaming herself and changing her friendliness and expressions of happiness would require *her* to take responsibility for this man's abusive behaviour. This did not fit with her ethics.

We also noted that Anna had many friendships with men that were not construed as sexual. These were exceptions to the dominant narrative that had emerged that "I must be naïve to think that I can be friendly towards men and for it not to be read as an invitation to have sex". Anna had approached her workplace HR manager and was told that nothing could be done about his comments on social media or his behaviour at work. Anna told me that despite not feeling confident to share this story with others after the response from HR, she had managed recently to tell her mother. Anna said that sharing the story with her mother had been helpful.

Thinking about her family's local knowledge and responses to difficult situations, Anna said that a saying of her father's was relevant here: "Just because someone gives you shoes doesn't mean you have to wear them." When I enquired about the meaning of this saying to Anna and her current situation, she said, "I don't need to take on other people's responsibility".

Towards the end of our conversation, I shared with Anna some of Elle's story of sexual assault in the workplace, as described in Chapter 6. I described Elle's sense of not knowing how to react when the director touched her under the table, and her experience of self-blame. We also spoke about the complexity that occurs when abuse takes place at work, as it had for Elle in the theatre and Anna in a government agency. I let Anna know that Elle had given me permission to speak with others about her experiences as a way of breaking the silence and offering solidarity to other women. Anna told me that it was really helpful to hear that Elle had also not known how to respond in the moment and had blamed herself for the man's actions, but that she had recently questioned self-blame and looked at issues of power. Anna said that this made her feel less alone and supported her questioning of self-blame.

In the business, retail and hospitality worlds, women are invited to surveil themselves: to monitor how they dress and interact. To appear professional, there is an expectation that women will wear makeup to look attractive but not too attractive, wear sophisticated clothing that is "feminine" but not too revealing, and be friendly and approachable but not too friendly and approachable. In Anna's story and the stories of some other women I have met with, sexual harassment in the workplace, either from customers or colleagues, is sometimes seen as a result of women getting this balance wrong. This makes the power tactics of sexual harassment invisible and has women blaming themselves.

In "Deconstruction and therapy" (1992), Michael White discussed Foucault's ideas about modern power and "the many practices of self and practices of relationships" (M. White, 1992, p. 136) that people are invited into. Some of the features of this system of power are that the source of power is invisible to the people most affected by it, and those affected are isolated in their experiences of being influenced and controlled by operations of power. People then take up monitoring and evaluating themselves in order to be acceptable to the (invisible) system. Anna had become convinced that she had been naïve in her approach to workplace relationships and had "failed" to fit what is expected of professional women. Through our deconstruction of these messages, the tactics of power that her male colleague had been using became more evident. He was diverting attention away from his own inappropriate and abusive actions by blaming her.

In our next conversation, Anna told me about some steps she had taken in the past fortnight in speaking with others about what had happened in her previous job. Anna reflected that speaking with others had her feeling less isolated. She told a male colleague whose response was supportive, and they came up with some humorous strategies to respond if something similar happened in the future. She said, "He made me laugh, and the knot in my stomach eased". She also spoke to a female friend who had been through something similar, and she too had tried to respond "politely". They were curious about Anna having apologised to the man for any "misunderstanding". They wondered why, as confident women, they felt a need to blame themselves and apologise to men who were using sexual harassment in the workplace. I asked some deconstruction questions to help Anna uncover the forces at play.

Loretta: What is it about being in a workplace, or in that workplace in particular, that had you wanting to "smooth things over" and take the action of apologising to him once you'd heard about the lies he was spreading?

Anna: I think it is quite hard to know how to respond to a colleague. It is different to responding to someone who is being rude or making sexist comments in a public space. We had an existing relationship as colleagues, so I had to be careful how I responded. There was a need to have an ongoing relationship. I knew I would see him every day and needed to be on the same team for certain projects. Our workplace valued "a cohesive team". I couldn't afford for it to be awkward.

Loretta: Do you think he was aware of this need you might experience to avoid awkwardness? Was it a trap? Given he had been spreading lies about you among the team and putting negative posts about you on social media, do you think there was any intentionality in him targeting someone in the workplace?

Anna: I guess he didn't like that I rejected him, and so he turned on me. But yes, there is a power that he had in terms of awkwardness in the workplace and my need to smooth things over. He had the boss's confidence, so if he wanted to, he could have said negative things about me generally to the boss as a way to undermine my position at work. This also made me think that if I pushed it further with HR, he would be more likely to be believed than me. When women put in a complaint, or push back against inappropriate behaviour, we are seen as "over reacting".

Loretta: So this helps us understand why you felt the need to smooth things over. What about your friend's comment about confident women feeling the need to apologise to men? It sounded like you were both speaking about it as a pattern bigger that the two of you. Also, your comment about women being seen to be "over reacting" sounds like it affects many women in society. In addition to what you have already described about the specific work context, what more broadly has women or girls feeling that they need to apologise when a man or boy wrongs them?

Anna: We are taught to be smaller than a man. We have to be lower. We are told that men don't like being overshadowed by women.

Loretta: What gives this message?

Anna: Conversations with friends, films, media. I saw a movie about Coco Chanel a few years ago. She was treated badly in a relationship, and later as she became more successful, she was seen as being "too big for her boots". We are taught that men feel intimidated if women are highly educated or have a higher income than their male partner or colleagues. Plus, in my field there are a lot of men. People express surprise at my education and skillset. These particular skills are seen to be "male traits", so some men don't like having a woman in a senior role. The old Jane Austen rules still apply, even though we think we have moved on.

We then discussed other films about famous women's lives and the common thread of women who experience commercial or artistic success being seen as "too big for their boots". This connected with Anna's sense that some men are intimidated by women who earn more money than them or have a higher status job. I asked Anna about the specific rules and customs highlighted in Jane Austen's novels and which of these had changed and which still existed. We also looked at characteristics that are valued in Western capitalist societies, such as independence, self-discipline, self-sufficiency, competitiveness and mathematical prowess, as being more encouraged in men, and being valued only up to a point in women. There seemed to be a tipping point at which women who are strong in these areas are seen as being too masculine. Anna's insight was that although there had been societal change, the reality of women's experience is that many of these old attitudes linger.

Utilising current news events and popular culture as a scaffolding tool

Engaging people in extended conversations about popular culture, such as films and songs, or about news events or podcasts, is a practice I have been developing over several years. However, it is linked to existing practices in narrative therapy. These include: externalising conversations that seek to situate the problem in its social and political contexts; use of deconstruction questions (M. White, 1992); and drawing on proverbs, sayings and common-sense understandings from "folk psychology" (Bruner, 1990; see M. White, 2001). Folk psychology assists us to make sense of the world according to community ideas about how people behave and why. Anna understood that "men don't like it when women have more status than them" through comments from other women, movies, books and understandings of Western cultural history. These cultural resources supported her to understand her own experiences. Therefore, use of films, songs and current news events to explore a person's own experience and deconstruct it through a lens of examining current and historical culture is a practice that I bring to scaffold conversations, taking the person from the "known and familiar" to "the possible to know" (Vygotsky, 1986, as cited in M. White, 2007, p. 271). It is a collaborative process: both Elle and Anna raised various films, newspaper reports and books, and I asked questions about what was important to them in these, and what I needed to understand to better appreciate their own stories. Together we examined how these popular culture artefacts could scaffold their understanding and meaning-making even further. The popular culture pieces and news reports assisted them to see their experiences as reflecting patriarchy's influence on society, rather than being isolated events. This assisted both Elle and Anna to step away from self-blame.

Use of folk psychology can also illuminate ways forward, positioning the person as an active participant in their own life and community, creating a sense of human agency – both personal agency and agency as a collective (M. White, 2001). For Anna and for Elle, hearing other women's stories and sharing their own stories with other women made them feel stronger as members of a collective. When speaking with Anna recently to assist me in writing up this experience, she identified that speaking with me and hearing about Elle had made her feel less alone, which in turn helped her speak with other women, only to discover that workplace sexual harassment was a common experience. She said, "I felt like I was the only one who had had such an experience and hence by default I must have 'triggered' it somehow". Anna then shared a story with me.

A few months after we had spoken, I managed to find an incredible kind and supportive boss and team, including a lot of strong and empowered women. At some point during a morning tea, a young junior analyst in my team made a remark about how grateful she was that I had hired her, as she had a really uncomfortable encounter in her last workplace and was "desperate" to get out of there. She mentioned how much it inspired her to work for such a "strong personality who does not let others take advantage of her". I had a good chuckle at that comment later on! Being able to tell her that she was not alone and nothing that had happened was in any way her fault by telling her briefly about my experience really seemed to have helped her come to terms with her story as well. I am so glad and grateful you encouraged me to try to verbalise and communicate the experience I had, so that now I can reach out to others as well.

The experience of connecting Anna with Elle's story, and Anna then speaking with female colleagues and discovering that workplace sexual harassment and assault were common experiences, echoes for me the stories of second-wave feminists sharing stories and realising that their experiences were not unique, but rather part of a pattern.[29] This awareness grew in relation to family and domestic violence, sexual assault, sexual harassment, unequal distribution of labour in the home, and gender-based discrimination in the workplace and broader society (Dwyer, Campey, & Foxworthy, 2020; Hill, 2019; C. White, 2016a). According to Hush (2020), prior to the consciousness-raising groups of the 1970s, rape was not considered to be common, and it was during these conversations with each other that women discovered how pervasive it is. Other social movements have been sparked by similar steps towards sharing previously unspoken experiences, developing solidarity and taking action.

In this work with Anna, I drew on a number of narrative practices underpinned by feminist principles:

- sharing stories among women of their responses to abuse and oppression (Crenshaw, 1991; Hare-Mustin, 1994; hooks, 2014; C. White, 2016a)

- deconstructing systems of power and messages women receive that uphold these (Lorde, 1984; Reynolds, 2014; M. White, 1992)

- making visible and naming tactics of power (hooks, 2014; Loveday, 2009; McPhie & Chaffey, 2000)

- bringing forward local knowledge from friends and family networks in responding to tactics of power (M. White, 1997)

- encouraging the person to connect with their networks rather than focusing on the counsellor/client relationship (a decentred but influential position)

- supporting further action in line with the person's principles and values.

---

[29] Cheryl White (2016a) described the significance of consciousness raising to the development of narrative practice. However, it is important to also note the experiences that were and were not included in this idea of a "shared pattern" in women's experience. (See for example hooks, 1984, 2014; Mohanty, 2003).

Additionally, a practice that I demonstrated in the stories of Elizabeth, Elle and Anna is collaboratively examining and utilising current news events and popular culture – podcasts, news reports, films, songs – as a scaffolding tool.

A groundswell of support for workplace reform

Feminist movements have been raising issues of sexual violence and harassment and other forms of oppression and injustice for decades. Following on from the #Me Too movement, which informed my work with Elle, there has been a resurgence of energy and passion for bringing forward gender equality, cultural change and justice, through which various social movements have found a voice and an audience. Such activist work influences the contexts in which experiences take place, and suggests possibilities for imagining further collective action.

In Australia in January 2020, the Sex Discrimination Commissioner, Kate Jenkins, handed the *Respect@Work* report about workplace sexual harassment and assault (Australian Human Rights Commission, 2020) to the Australian Government. It has since been made publicly available. In this report, Jenkins cited a survey by the Australian Human Rights Commission (2018), which found that one in three people had experienced sexual harassment at work in the previous five years. The report also stated that Aboriginal and Torres Strait Islander people were more likely (53%) to be subjected to workplace sexual harassment compared to non-Indigenous people (32%). With women being subjected to sexual harassment at a higher rate (39%) than men (26%), the intersection of race and gender means that First Nations women experience a heightened risk of workplace sexual harassment. Unless we find ways in our practice to explore these intersections, First Nations people may be left with a belief that their experience of sexual harassment is an isolated event and they are somehow to blame.

Despite the prevalence of workplace sexual harassment and assault, Elle, Anna and Anna's colleagues had all been invited into a sense of isolation and self-blame. This demonstrates that linking their stories to the broader context through sharing high-profile stories or stories from people we meet with is important in addressing this isolation and self-blame and move towards solidarity.

Political and legal inaction have long frustrated Australian women. A groundswell of support for an end to sexual violence erupted in thousands taking to the streets on 15 March 2021 for the March 4 Justice across dozens of locations in Australia.[30] Following the March 4 Justice and continued pressure in the media, the government finally released its response to the *Respect@Work* report, more than a year after receiving it. There will be significant changes to the federal Fair Work Act and the Sex Discrimination Act. One of the reforms will be that members of parliament, judges and state public servants will be liable for and protected from sexual harassment in the workplace ("Politicians and judges to be included", 2021). They had previously been exempted from the Sex Discrimination Act. The law across all workplaces will change to include sexual harassment as grounds for dismissal. Another change will be working more actively towards prevention, aiming for cultural change through education, training and research ("Politicians and judges to be included", 2021). I look forward to seeing these changes and discussing them with the women I meet with through my work. I am hopeful that I will hear anecdotal reports of a decrease in workplace sexual harassment and assault, and better reporting systems and responses from employers when it does occur. Most people who I speak to about workplace sexual harassment are simply wanting the harassment to stop, and for their employer to demonstrate that they "have my back" by telling the person to stop, or by preventing the person from being promoted, or by dismissing the person. They want others to be prevented from suffering what they have suffered. Some also want acknowledgment of the harm done.

****

Without discussing the power issues involved in workplace sexual harassment and assault, and how this links to the broader context of misogyny,

---

[30] One of the precipitating events was former federal political staffer Brittany Higgins alleging that she had been raped by a colleague in Parliament House. Higgins reported this to her employer but was not given adequate support. The staffer denied the allegations. Some women have told me that they were left feeling that if the people making our laws are not even going to protect their own staff, then women throughout Australia cannot be safe at work.

women can be left with a sense of isolation and self-blame. This chapter has demonstrated the use of deconstruction and of drawing on current news events and popular culture to explore attitudes and social structures that support patriarchy and misogyny as possible ways to address isolation and self-blame. Current news events and popular culture can also be highlighted to celebrate acts of resistance and solidarity made in the social and political spheres. Anna's story also demonstrated how these therapeutic conversations can support women to connect with colleagues and family, creating support networks. The next chapter further discusses using deconstruction and current news events and social media in the context of conversations about sexual assault by peers among high-school and university students.

Reflection

- Are you hearing references to current news events or popular culture in your therapeutic conversations?

- Are you using these as a scaffolding tool, or is this something you might try?

- These stories included conversations about sites of power and actions of harm by those in positions of power. What do you currently do to make visible the systems of power that people are up against?

- Is there something additional that you would like to say or do in future?

9.
Working towards cultural change and against sexual assault on campus

There is a long and rich history of grassroots feminist activists raising their voices about sexual harassment and sexual assault in schools, university campuses and on-campus accommodation (often called "colleges"). This activism has included calling on schools and universities to provide education to reduce gender-based violence, to provide support services to respond to those who have been assaulted, and to implement clear policies and procedures for reporting sexual harassment and sexual assault. Feminist abolitionists such as Erica Meiners (2011) in the US have also drawn attention to the importance of making schools and universities safe while avoiding carceral responses.

This chapter includes stories from women in Australia who have been subjected to sexual assault by school or university peers, and those who stand as allies with them in working for cultural change. In other countries there is also much work being done in relation to sexual harassment and sexual assault in schools and universities, such as the work of narrative practitioner Shelja Sen (2021) in India, who supports young women to explore gender-based discourses that lead to sexual harassment, and recognises their efforts to respond to these forces and to move in their preferred directions in life. There is also work being done to support young men to form respectful ways of being in relationships to reduce gender-based violence (Wishart & Maeder, 2018).

This chapter will further demonstrate the use of deconstruction and drawing on current news events and popular culture, as well as exploring the absent-but-implicit values, beliefs and commitments in expressions of outrage, and the actions that flow from these values, beliefs and commitments. The importance of collective action in working towards cultural change is also explored.

Bella's story

Bella is a white woman who was 20 years old at the time we were meeting. She was studying at university and living on campus. Her parents were providing emotional and financial support for her studies. Bella's hope for our sessions was to reduce the effects of anxiety in her life. At the start of our second conversation, Bella described her distress and outrage that a student who also lived on campus had been raped at a local nightclub. Bella asked if we could focus on this, rather than just discussing anxiety. She spoke about the harmful response from police and security at the club, and we discussed the link with societal views about women who drink alcohol. Bella had heard that the police who interviewed the woman who was raped at the club asked questions such as "How much were you drinking?" Bella named this as victim shaming, and we explored her knowledge of this shaming practice, drawing on news reports, books and discussions with friends. We both knew people who had encountered harmful responses from police. These experiences challenge the discourse that calling the police or security will provide safety and that the person who used violence will be held to account by the "criminal justice" system.

Then we discussed issues of consent and a recent effort by university campuses across Australia to provide education about consent at the start of every student's university education. Bella said that her university had implemented a consent module that had to be completed by all students. She told me that this module included ideas such as looking out for one another and that a person can say "no" to sexual contact at any point, even during sex. The introduction of this module was in response to stories emerging of the high number of sexual assaults that happen on campuses and in university accommodation.

In 2017, the Australian Human Rights Commission (2017b) released a report on sexual violence on campus and provided detailed information to each university about the prevalence of sexual assault among their students. The report also recommended changes to university policies and procedures, with specific actions to better safeguard students and support those who have been assaulted. The current attention to this issue has been made possible in part by "decades of work by campus-based feminist activists who sought to expose the ingrained culture of abuse and harassment that permeated Australian universities" (Hush, 2020, p. 293). How might we take hold of this momentum of social movement action and bring the social context into our work? I ask people what they are noticing that connects their story with other stories in the media, or with what they know of current or past social movements. I invite reflections on changes that are occurring and what still needs to happen. This provides space for the person to reflect on their own role in society, and actions they are taking or might choose to take that fit with their beliefs and values. In joining voices and experiences together, people develop a sense of solidarity, which supports hope and sustainability.

Example questions to explore and deconstruct responses from authorities

- What was the response from security or police when the assault was reported?

- What were the effects of this response on you (or, as in Bella's situation, the person who was assaulted)?

- What did you say or think to yourself in response to that harmful police response?

- What is your guess about the impact on others who witnessed or heard about this police response?

- What effect might this have on people seeking help from security or police in the future?

- What influences this attitude by security or police? Are there ideas in society that you think might be connected?

- You mentioned "victim shaming" (or other discourse). Where did you hear about this – from friends or in the news or social media?

- What does this phrase or idea mean to you?

- What is the history of this phrase or idea, do you think?

- Given that the police response was unhelpful, what other community-based responses can you imagine might be helpful?

Bella noted that other initiatives the university said it was taking hadn't yet happened. For example, on-campus security was supposed to be available to call in a crisis and was meant to provide an escort home if a student felt unsafe. The woman's friends called security when they discovered she had been raped, but the security officer reportedly said, "We will get there when we get there". Other students, including Bella, had found that when they called on-campus security for assistance, they were slow to respond or didn't turn up. I asked Bella about various ways she and other students had responded to this problem. She said that she had reported the problem to the university accommodation service. She also described a community-based response she and other senior residents had come up with: to give their own mobile numbers out to students in their buildings, so that students could get support at night to move around campus or seek help without relying on security services. I asked about the hopes, intentions and values connected to these actions. Bella spoke about her strong desire for people to be safe, and her belief that women have the right to be out in the community enjoying their lives. Bella and other senior residents had been advising and supporting younger students. However, Bella said the advice that she had given was a little at odds with her beliefs and values, focusing on ways to try to *keep yourself safe*, including being aware of drink spiking ("don't leave your drink unattended", "don't allow someone to buy you a drink") and travelling with friends rather than alone. I asked Bella what her preferred message would be, and she said to tell people "don't rape". Bella highlighted that the focus in society is often on ways women should behave to "keep themselves safe", which may imply that they have somehow failed if they are assaulted. Bella believed the focus should be on men taking responsibility for their own behaviour and supporting their friends to treat women with respect. She told me about various devices to detect drink spiking, which were being recommended to students. Bella said, "It is sad that it has come to that. Education should be about not raping, not about guarding your drink".

Bella expressed sadness, anger and disgust that this had happened to a woman from her accommodation block. When hearing strong emotions, this is a cue to consider asking about beliefs and values that sit in the background – about what is absent but implicit in these expressions (M. White, 2000b). When I asked about what the anger was in relation to, Bella articulated a belief: "It's 2019. This shouldn't be happening!" She spoke about the anger that came from knowing that even with the #MeToo movement making issues of sexual harassment and assault more prominent in people's minds, so many women saying "we won't stand for this", and the years of work of groups like End Rape on Campus, rape was still happening. She said, "Society is changing, but I just want rape to stop now!" She described a sense of "almost hopelessness" in the face of ongoing violence against women. This strong statement, and her experience of "almost hopelessness" gave me additional opportunities to explore the absent but implicit, and we were again able to traverse the rich landscape of Bella's hopes, values, beliefs and commitments, as well as actions Bella had taken in line with these.

Example questions to explore the absent but implicit

- What is it about this attack in particular that has you experiencing sadness?

- You said you are experiencing anger, and I could hear it in your voice. What is the anger in relation to?

- When you said, "Society is changing, but I just want rape to stop now!" I noticed your passion. Is "passion" the right word?

- When did you first start feeling this strongly about women's right to safety?

- When you say "almost hopelessness", does that mean there is a little piece of hope left, or is it something else?

- What is it that is driving back hopelessness and
  inviting a little bit of hope?

- Who else knows about this little bit of hope
  and supports you in keeping it alive?

Connections between personal stories and social movements

Bella spoke about the belief that things are changing and that she can be
part of that change. She recalled various moments that had encouraged her,
such as the way former Australian Prime Minister Julia Gillard had called
out misogyny in parliament.[31] This opened the way for me to ask about the
steps she and others were taking as a result of this hope and the belief that
things are changing. We discussed that she can be, and already is, a part of
that change. Bella spoke about university events she and others had helped
organise to support men to explore what's meant by "toxic masculinity" and
to find other ways to be a man. It brought her hope, seeing that men were
working together with women to host this event. Bella spoke about being
an active bystander, calling people to account for their sexist jokes, or jokes
that condone sexual assault. She spoke about the importance of being a
good friend to other women and being supported by other women – a two-
way flow. Bella also said she had been initiating friendships with younger
students and making herself available to listen. This had resulted in young
women speaking to her about their experiences of unsafe and disrespectful
relationships, and about sexual harassment and assault. Bella had been able
to offer assurance, care and referral to appropriate services. Above all, she
said, the young women appreciated that she believed them.

In the back of my mind as we were discussing these things were some
songs I had heard on the radio. I mentioned to Bella that I had heard in
recent years songs by female singer-songwriters challenging the culture of

---

[31] The famous "misogyny speech" occurred in parliament in 2012 while Julia Gillard was
serving as Prime Minister. Gillard was the first and as yet the only female prime minister
of Australia. She has since written several books, including editing the feminist collection,
Not now, not ever: Ten years on from the misogyny speech (Gillard, 2022). In this book,
Gillard reported a conversation with three young Australian activists, Chanel Contos,
Caitlin Figueiredo and Sally Scales, who described their hopes for cultural change and the
steps they were taking to help achieve this.

sexual harassment and assault, and a song by a man who was telling other men that if a woman is too drunk to walk, then she is too drunk to give consent. We wondered together about whether cultural change is making such songs more common, or whether the songs are supporting culture to change, or whether it is happening in both directions.

In circling back to the reason Bella had originally come to see me, we were both happily surprised that anxiety had not overtaken Bella since she had heard about the rape. We explored the ways she had been taking care of herself, which anxiety did not like, such as staying connected to friends, getting some exercise, and pausing and assessing an anxious thought. It was useful for Bella to notice anxiety's intentions, such as keeping her in her room, and then decide if this was the direction she wanted her life to go in.

In place of hopelessness, Bella chose to focus on "What can I do now?" She thought about further steps she could take on campus, such as shutting down victim-shaming rumours in relation to the recent assault, and instead opening up further conversations about mutual support and solidarity among people of all genders. She could invite other senior residents to also be on the lookout for inappropriate jokes or rumours. This was part of our discussion about ways Bella could stay connected to the movement to end gendered violence, rather than take it on as her responsibility alone (which might fit more with anxiety's agenda of making her responsible for everything). This sparked the idea of following up with the university again *as a group of senior residents* about the security issues and other aspects of addressing sexual assault, such as clear reporting guidelines and support for people who have been subjected to assault. However, reporting to the university and police is not a *solution* to the problem of violence. The experiences I have heard from people on the receiving end of violence is that reporting has not achieved what they have desired in terms of justice or healing. This has me thinking about what else might be possible.

Since this conversation, I have been introduced to abolitionist feminist ideas, which invite us to reimagine a society that doesn't rely on police or security guards to prevent violence or respond to violence. In this reimagined society, meeting local community needs, preventing violence, and reducing inequality would be prioritised, enabling people to live well and safely. Support would be envisioned and enacted by the local community. People who use violence would be held to account, but without resorting to state violence as a response (A. Y. Davis, Dent, Meiners, & Richie, 2022). Reflecting on my conversation with Bella, I appreciate her efforts to provide a safe space for people to speak about their experiences and be believed and supported. I also appreciate the efforts of her campus community to collaborate across gender to change culture to reduce and hopefully end sexual violence.

Example questions to draw a connection between a personal story and a social movement

- What is it like to hear about similar stories from friends, in the media or on social media? (This could be asked through separate questions or choose the most relevant)

- Does hearing about this from others offer you something useful, such as a sense of not being alone in the experience or that others understand?

- Do you remember the name of someone who shared their story? Or can you tell me what you remember of their story?

- What stands out to you about this story?

- How does it connect with your story or the concern we have been discussing?

- When you hear people speaking of their own experience to the media, does this make it harder or easier to speak with your friends about your experience? Or perhaps it makes no difference or a bit of both?

- When you hear people speaking in the media, such as [Brittany Higgins, Grace Tame[32] or whomever the person relates to in their

---

[32] Grace Tame is an Australian activist advocating for survivors of sexual assault, especially in relation to law reform. She uses the hashtag #LetHerSpeak. Grace Tame was named Australian of the Year in 2021. As mentioned in the previous chapter, Brittany Higgins alleged that she was raped by a colleague in Parliament House and reported this to her employer. She has spoken out about the treatment of people reporting sexual offences and the failure of the "criminal justice" system to deliver an adequate response.

own culture], does it support hope, or a move towards action, or something else?

- What would you call it? How would you describe this sense?

- You mentioned wanting to "take action"[33] – what changes would you like to see in our society?

- What might be your next step in this?

- Who are you already joining with, or who might you join with?

- In social movements, there is an idea that voices are stronger together. Does this connect with you in some way?

- Does it connect to other philosophies you believe in or social movements you are a part of or you respect (such as Black Lives Matter, the union movement, the Indigenous land rights movement)?

- In taking the steps you have already taken, or in thinking about potential steps, what value does this connect with?

- What is the history of this value in your life?

When I asked Bella about the history of her values and commitments, she said

> My values come from my family. I believe attitudes are learnt. All my life my mother and grandmother have asked me, "What kind of human being do you want to be? What effect do you want to have in this world?" So I've thought about this often, and the most important things to me are not about money or status, but about being kind, supporting people, and letting my family and friends know that they are loved. When I think about taking a step or not, or thinking about

---

[33] "Action" here is not meant to equate to speaking publicly about one's own experience. There are a range of actions that might be taken to connect with a social movement. There should be no agenda or pressure from the practitioner to take action or imply what that action might look like.

how to respond to a situation, this question helps me decide what to do – it keeps me accountable. "Who do I want to be?" It makes me focus on my values. I want to have a positive impact on the world, and so supporting women and helping men change their attitude is part of that.

Collective action to protest sexual violence

Recently, many young women have spoken out on social media about their experiences of sexual harassment at school and sexual assault at parties with other students from their school (or for those at single-sex schools, with students from their "brother" school). In Sydney, where I live, there have been a lot of stories from former students of elite private schools. There are wonderings about whether the large number of sexual assaults is caused by a lack of education about consent or whether there is a stronger sense of entitlement among private school boys due to class privilege (Leser & Chrysanthos, 2021). Some young people who have spoken to me say that some private school boys they know have a sense that they will be able to "get away with it" because their father is a lawyer or has plenty of money to pay a lawyer. One voice that has added a lot of momentum to the call for better education about consent and respectful relationships is Chanel Contos. Three days after federal staffer Brittany Higgins's allegations about being raped in Parliament House were made public, Contos started an online petition to address harassment and assault in schools. After hearing stories from multiple friends about being subjected to sexual assault, she initiated a petition for consent to be included in high-school sex education and established an online space[34] for young women to share their stories. In three weeks, she had garnered 30000 signatures and almost 5000 testimonies (Contos, 2021) from girls who were current or former students of elite private schools across Australia.

There has been criticism of the feminist movement for focusing on already privileged white middle-class or upper-class women, and for giving little support or attention to the experiences of interpersonal and state

---

[34] Teachusconsent.com

violence, oppression and marginalisation of women of colour (Huggins, 2022; Lorde, 1984; Moreton-Robinson, 2000). Most stories I am hearing in the media are from highly educated white middle-class or upper-class women. It seems that little has changed in terms of whose stories are told. When I speak to women who attended public (government-funded) schools, some of them have also experienced sexual assault at parties by school peers, and both women and men remember a culture of misogynistic language and actions by male students in public schools. In addition to the action that is being taken by private school students, public school students are also taking action. When recently in Adelaide, I read an article about female students from Adelaide High School who held a protest against what they perceived to be inaction by the school in response to reports of sexual harassment. One student was quoted as saying, "We should not have to walk through school halls to be told by male students daily what they will do to us sexually" (DiGirolamo, 2021). The stories are out there, and young people want to be heard.

These stories of sexual assault at parties or harassment by young men who are known to the young women reminded me of what Bella told me of discussions with her friends. Many of her friends described their first sexual experience in a way that raised red flags to Bella. What they were describing didn't sound to Bella like first-time sex, it sounded like assault. Her friends said things like, "He kept pressuring me", or "I wanted to leave but he didn't let me". As they discussed this, Bella and her friends were able to explore what constituted sexual assault, what consent means, and what actions are in line with the respect that they would want in a relationship. They were all horrified to realise how common sexual assault is, and that many young women don't know that pressured sex or sex when a woman is too affected by alcohol or drugs to consent is assault, or that assault from someone you know or trust is still assault. These conversations with her friends informed and fuelled Bella's passion to reach out to younger students.

Many young women have told me that the response from their friends after disclosing sexual assault has been significant to them. For women who were not believed, or who were blamed by their friends for the assault, the result was devastating and had made it much harder to speak to others. It hindered efforts to reclaim a sense of wellbeing. This doesn't mean that they won't find healing and justice, but that the road was made harder. In these situations, I am careful to explore how it was that they had managed to speak with me, despite these responses from others. What did it take to even consider booking the appointment? It might have taken courage or self-compassion. We might name this as "another step towards healing" or "an action of self-care" or "a step away from silencing". I also explore other avenues through which they have sought connection and validation, such as with family members or a different friend. Other connections might be with people they haven't met, such as through podcasts or books from those who have shared their story or taken action for the benefit of others.

I also acknowledge the sense of hurt and betrayal when their friend did not believe them or blamed them. This sense of hurt and betrayal is additional to the anguish and distress caused by the assault.

At times, a person who has been harmed wants to explore a bewildering and harmful response they received from friends or family members. The questions below are aimed at assisting the person to explore the social and political contexts of the response they received. The person may have received different responses from different people. The intention behind this is to separate the person from the problem. We are separating the friend or family member from internalising labels, just as we would for the "client". However, this certainly does not reduce the responsibility of the friend or family member for their response and the harm caused by this response. Nor are we aiming to convince the client that their friend or family member didn't really mean it or really does love them. It is a careful and gentle exploration, which should be guided by the hopes and intentions of the person who has been harmed. If they initiate a conversation about wanting to understand the response they received, then we can tentatively offer an exploration of the social and political context. It is important to note that the effects of this response would be explored first. Some example questions to explore the effects of the response are offered in Chapter 5. The relationship would also need to be evaluated for safety and the person might choose to upgrade or downgrade the status of the relationship using re-membering questions (M. White, 2007).

Sarah, whose story was mentioned in Chapter 5, wanted to understand why her mother had blamed her for being raped and why she physically assaulted her. This response had Sarah experiencing shame and self-hate, which led to an eating disorder. Our aim was not to move an internalised label from Sarah only to place a label on her mother, such as "terrible mother"; however, we did not excuse her mother's response. Sarah and I came to understand that her mother's own experience of being sexually assaulted and shamed and silenced may have shaped her response. Sarah said this was helpful to understand and *didn't* mean that what her mother did was okay. Sarah was able to navigate her relationship with her mother on her own terms, such as only seeing her mother for short periods. Prior to meeting up, Sarah would call first to check out her mother's current thinking, as her mother was also affected by schizophrenia.

Simone, whose story was shared in Chapter 5, was able to see that her husband's blaming and shaming response to her rape fit with his pattern of behaviour in the context of ongoing serious physical and emotional abuse. In the past she had been hospitalised due to his use of physical violence, and he had been verbally abusive to her just prior to her leaving the house on the evening of the rape. She had gone out to escape his verbal and emotional abuse. Seeing this response from him in the context of gendered intimate partner violence assisted in further discussion of options for Simone to consider in relation to leaving the relationship or putting in additional supports.

Similarly, a friend may also be using emotional abuse or more subtle undermining and manipulation tactics, which need to be explored at a suitable time. These responses often contribute to shame and self-blame, even if the person who was assaulted usually believes that a person who has been assaulted is not at fault.

Some questions to try to make sense of a harmful response from friends or family members

- Would you be interested in putting self-blame and shame to the side for the moment, and seeing what might be another way to understand this person's response?

- What reason might there possibly be for your friend or family member to deny that X assaulted you?

- Why might they prefer to think that it didn't happen or that it was consensual?

- You said that believing you might require them to change their opinion of that person. Why might they not be open to changing their opinion of that person?

- You've come up with some possible answers (e.g. they would then have to decide whether or not to change their relationship with the person; they might be expected to support me to go to the police, and they don't want their friend/relative to be harmed by the carceral system; it would burst the bubble of their image of having the perfect family; they might feel they have let me down because they couldn't protect me). What is it like to consider these possibilities?

- Do you think there was anything else happening that might change over time, such as initial shock or uncertainty about how to respond? Have they said or done anything since that makes you think they might regret their initial response?

- When this person you love blamed you or minimised what happened, do you think they were buying into an idea or message they had heard somewhere else (e.g. women need to be more careful; men can't help themselves if women wear short skirts)? Are there bigger forces at play than just you and them (gender-based violence; male privilege etc.)?

- Does this person's blaming and minimising response fit with what you know of them? Have there been other times when they have blamed or shamed you or others or undermined you or others?

- Is this type of response common in the relationship, or does this really stand out as being an anomaly, an unusual response from them?

If the person states that they are often undermined or blamed by this person, or they express other concerns about the relationship, this should be explored in further detail. It may be a sign that they are being subjected to manipulative practices or coercive control. This can happen in friendships, families or intimate relationships. We might say, "You've said this undermining has happened quite often. Can you tell me about another one of these times?" Then we might ask, "Given that this has happened multiple times, would you be willing for us to take a closer look at the ways this person is treating you and the impact of this?" It can be a slow process to help someone explore the relationship and support them to evaluate its safety. The idea of concept development was discussed in Chapter 4 and can assist in exploring such ideas as trust, respect, love and really getting into the details of what these look like, as compared to actions that have been labelled as love but are used to manipulate or control the person. Following the statement of position map 1 (M. White, 2007) will lead to an evaluation question about the manipulative practices or the undermining. We can then ask evaluative questions about the relationship itself, and whether or not the person wants to step away from the relationship.

For those who were believed and supported by friends, this made a positive difference to their sense of themselves and to their healing journey.[35] Representations on TV and in movies in which the woman screams or repeatedly says "no" mean that women who were affected by drugs or alcohol, or who were in a freeze state, sometimes feel that their response was inadequate. They may doubt whether what happened can be classified as assault.

Olivia came to speak with me about the ongoing effects of a sexual assault that had occurred at a party, when the effects of alcohol meant that she was unable to walk or talk. Despite experiencing negative physical sensations and emotional responses that fit with her understanding of trauma, Olivia said that at times she got confused about the assault. I asked her what the confusion says or does to confuse her. Olivia said that due to the effects of alcohol, parts of her memory were unclear, so confusion suggested that maybe she wasn't remembering it accurately. We then discussed alcohol and consent, and she was very clear that if someone can't walk or talk then they are too drunk to say "yes" or to fully understand what is going on, so therefore there is no consent. I asked her what this understanding does to

---

[35] For a more thorough discussion on drawing on friendships as a community response to injustice with women who have survived sexual assault, see Dang (2018).

confusion. Olivia said that this helps her know that she was too drunk to give consent, which makes confusion evaporate. We also spoke about the ways she responded to try to protect herself, despite not being able to stop him. Another key thought was that her friends came to find her, and they witnessed her distress and they yelled at him to get away from her. In times of confusion, she drew on this memory of her friends' response immediately after the assault. They came to find Olivia because they knew she was unsafe. They saw her distress, which confirmed that it was not consensual. They yelled at him. I asked her what meaning she took from this, and she said that her friends could immediately see that it was sexual assault, and they were angry at him. She stated that although the assault had negative consequences, such as nightmares, panic, anger outbursts and difficulties with physical intimacy, the knowledge that her friends yelled at the young man who assaulted her comforted her. It made her feel cared for and supported. It also cut through the confusion around alcohol and consent. In recent times, Olivia had told her father about the sexual assault, and he had responded with care and support. Using re-membering questions (M. White, 2007), I was able to assist Olivia to acknowledge the values and the attributes she and her father shared. She enjoyed honouring her dad in our conversation, acknowledging the effects of his care, and considering herself as similar to him. We also discussed the ways Olivia had contributed to the lives of her father and her friends to resist the idea that she was a burden to them. Dang (2018) has taken this a step further, exploring the way the actions taken by supportive family or friends to respond to an assault or to challenge the aspects of culture that make sexual assault possible may also contribute to the friends' own sense of self or to their relationships.

****

When having conversations with women about sexual assault, I see my role as moving beyond listening well and contributing to healing. I invite contemplation about broader issues of gender-based violence and injustice, and then support connection with other women, either through their own networks, or through sharing stories of knowledge, skills and resistance among the women I have met through my work. These various aspects of the work provide a foundation for local social movement (Denborough, 2008). Some women are already very familiar with thinking about broader issues of injustice and placing their experiences in this context, but for others this is new. Some, like Bella, are already connecting and sharing their skills and knowledges and experiencing a sense of contribution to others, in which case, I hope our conversations fan the flame.

Reflection

- Which story in this chapter did you connect with the most? What was it about this story that resonated for you or challenged you in some way?

- What has this got you thinking about?

- What might be different for you or for the people you meet with on account of hearing these stories?

- What small action will you take on account of hearing these stories and being inspired or offered healing or challenged (or something else)?

10.
Spirituality and narrative practice

This chapter offers examples of practices that explore ways people who have been assaulted have survived the assault and ways they are reclaiming their lives from trauma. The focus of this chapter is on inviting conversations that open space for recognition of the role that faith and spirituality can have in people's sense of identity and in their process of surviving and reclaiming life after a traumatic event. There is particular attention drawn to increasing a sense of agency for those who felt they were passive in their journey of survival.

I would like to start this chapter by situating myself in terms of my history with religion and spirituality. I was born into a Catholic family, but by the time I was six, my mother had left the Catholic church and over time we attended various Protestant churches. My father had become an atheist, and we had lots of rigorous discussions about the Bible, science and faith. Growing up in a church environment, I have experienced sacred moments and supportive community. I have also witnessed abuses of power within the church and in Christian schools. I have heard many stories of harm and many stories of support, community, tenderness and healing. I also know that spirituality can be separated out from religion, or from the actions of those who have caused harm. Spirituality can be understood to have different meanings and different shapes.

Deconstruction

With these different threads in my hand, narrative practice and the philosophies that underpin it have felt like a good way to weave these experiences and understandings together. I can hold both critique and appreciation. I can step further back or closer in to examine the threads and the tapestry.

Although deconstruction questions open up space to examine power, in narrative practice these explorations are not pushy or disrespectful. We are not persuading people one way or another, but gently creating a safe space for the person to consider the operations of power they have been subject to. This often is seen through expectations on their life, and we can ask about the way family, society or religion may have influenced those expectations. For those who have attended a religious school or boarding school, grown up in an institutional "care" home or lived in a tight-knit religious community or in a cult, these practices of power may be even more influential, as they stretch beyond the daily influence of family and beyond the weekly influences of church, synagogue, temple or mosque. I appreciate that deconstruction offers an opportunity for people to consider what is working well for them and what is perhaps not as useful.

With reflective practice we are encouraged to examine these influences on ourselves as practitioners and to question our own use of power in the counselling room or community space. A decentred posture has us valuing the perspectives of the people we meet with and respecting their right to agency over their own lives. We can welcome people of all faiths or no faith and hear their stories with respect.

Example questions for practitioner self-reflection[36]

- Which aspects of religion or spirituality do I treasure?

- Which aspects of religion or spirituality have I found unhelpful?

- Which aspects of religion might be less visible to me?

---

[36] For those who are atheists, reflection questions might also consider the influence of atheism as a belief system.

- Are there negative effects for others in the community caused by the beliefs and actions of a religious or spiritual community I am a part of?

- Which cultures or subcultures do I belong to?

- Which aspects of culture might be less visible to me?

- Are there ideas or beliefs I am "swimming in" on a daily basis that I have not yet examined?

- What are the effects of these on the way I am hearing this person's story?

- When I feel a sense of discomfort about what a person has said, what is that discomfort connected to?

- Is this connected to a value I hold or that my religion or culture holds?

- Is there a difference between my values and the values of my religion or culture in relation to this issue? If so, does this mean I need to change my values or hold them more closely?

- In work, or in my time outside of work, when I experience a random thought that doesn't fit with my values, what does this mean? Does this mean that I am not living according to my values? Or does it mean that I am perhaps being influenced by some dominant ideas in society?

- Is this something I need to reflect further on?

- Does it require some action?

Re-authoring and re-membering

In re-authoring and re-membering (M. White, 2007), we are tracing the history of values, beliefs, principles and commitments, and honouring and celebrating those people who have made a rich contribution to our lives and the lives of those we are meeting with. We are supporting people to consider how they have contributed to the lives of others. We are collaborating to uncover what assists people to get through hard times. For some, connecting with the sacred is an important part of meaning-making. During the worst times, faith can even support people in a struggle for survival. My life experiences and the different perspectives of members of my family have supported my curiosity in these arenas.

Agency and spirituality

During times of danger and harm, many people find spiritual beliefs, and their relationship to God, their spiritual teacher and/or their faith community, to be highly significant and sustaining. For others, they may have felt a distance from God or their community of faith during this hard time. We can be curious about the situation, events, actions and thoughts that led up to this, and the meaning that the person has drawn from either of these experiences.

I have met with people who have been kidnapped and raped, or who were assaulted during a date and then threatened with murder. Often there is a strong sense of shame and distress about the assault. Among other aspects of the work, it has been significant to acknowledge that in order for the person to be here speaking with me today, they must have somehow escaped. For some, as we have discussed their escape, they have expressed a belief that God assisted them and their gratitude about this. Such a belief can be significantly comforting. While wanting to honour this, I have noticed that for some, it can erase any sense of agency. For some, the idea that God helped them escape does not reduce the sense of shame.

Riley's story

When I met Riley, she was 25 years old and was wanting to reduce the effects of anxiety in her life. In exploring her hopes for her life, she said she had already achieved some goals: finishing university and moving interstate. She wanted to "meet someone" and eventually get married and have children but said that anxiety was making it hard for her to go on dates. She was concerned that a man might seem to be nice, but that he might be just pretending. Riley also said that anxiety was making her very stressed about having children, as the world is not safe, and she might not be able to protect them. In tracing the history of these fears, Riley told me that five years earlier, she had been held captive and repeatedly sexually assaulted by someone she had trusted. He had tricked her into moving to Australia with the promise of a job. His hidden intention was to sell her into sexual slavery. She was struggling with a sense of worthlessness and shame and stated that she did not believe she was deserving of a good life. I asked her how she had escaped. Riley told me that God had provided a way for her to escape. She told me that she had always known that God loved her. She stated that without God's intervention, she would not have escaped. I wondered how I might honour her faith and gratitude to God, and also bring forward a conversation about Riley's agency in her own life.

Below I have listed some questions that I used to explore Riley's relationship with God and the circumstances of the escape. The questions draw on the concept that people always respond to traumatic or oppressive situations (as discussed in Chapters 5 and 6; also see Wade, 1997; M. White, 1995a). The questions about spiritual beliefs, songs, scriptures and the history of these are drawn from Denborough (2008). For readers trying out the questions listed throughout this book, keep in mind that questions should be shaped by the person's responses, and not all questions would need to be used. Using the questions included here, the conversation may extend across two or three sessions as we build the picture of God's support and the person's own agency. Connection to others is also important.

My questions to Riley were shaped by various intentions:

- to respect and honour her faith

- to support the development of a sense of agency
  while respecting God's contribution to the escape

- to explore or build a support team

- to deconstruct self-blame

- to make visible that responsibility sits with the person who kidnapped and sexually assaulted her

- to find out more about Riley's meaning-making

- to explore how Riley had continued to reclaim her life after this horrendous ordeal.

Supporting agency and respecting faith: Questions eliciting responses

- How did you survive the horrendous ordeal you have described? Were there things you did, or thoughts you had, to make it a little more bearable?

- Were there things you did to protect your mind, body or spirit in some way?

- Can you tell me how you escaped? What did you do?

- How did you think to do that, despite being so frightened?

- What was your hope or intention in doing that?

- Had you been planning it for a while, or was it a spontaneous break for freedom?

- Had you previously tried to escape? Was this possibly useful knowledge gathering for when you finally escaped, or would you describe it another way?

- You said God gave you the opportunity to escape, and that it was his[37] plan you followed. How did you know that he was indicating this to you? Did it sound like a voice or a thought, or did he show you a sign?

- Do you have a history of listening to God?

---

[37] In respecting the person's beliefs, we can listen out for how they refer to God or other spiritual figures, including what names and pronouns they use.

- Would you describe it as a dialogue between you, or is it more like God speaks and you listen?

- I'm assuming you could have chosen not to take the opportunity that God provided, or that you could have been too scared to take it. Would you say that you had to take a step, some sort of action to escape?

- What would you call these steps that you took to put God's plan into action?

- What did it take – courage, trust in God or something else?

- Is there something you know from your own experience or from the Bible[38] that helped you know that you could trust God?

- What did you do after you escaped?

Further developing the sense that God is on Riley's team: Re-membering questions

- What might God be appreciating about how you placed your trust in him at that time?

- Do you think it is meaningful to God when people trust him? What might it mean to him?

- Is there another story of a time you took action and God was with you, or when he showed you the way and you trusted him?

- If we think of your life as being a club with invited members (M. White, 2007)[39], would you describe God as being in your club or on your team?

- How long has God been on your team?

---

[38] We can ask which sacred text is important to the person.

[39] We can offer the metaphors of a "club of life" or "support team" and see which has more resonance for the person.

- If you were to see yourself through God's loving eyes at the time of the kidnapping and your escape, what do you think he would be seeing that perhaps was not visible to you?

- You said your family was unsympathetic and unsupportive after your ordeal. What is it like knowing that God was loving you and supporting you at that time?

- You said God has continued to support you. Were you aware of his love and support during that difficult year after your escape, even though you felt let down by other people, or is that a newer realisation looking back?

- Even though you felt let down by some people, were there others who did support you, or who stood by you?

- Would you say that these people are in your support team?

Riley and I explored these ideas over three sessions. She realised that she had chosen to listen to God, and that she had a long history of identifying his voice and separating it out from "just thoughts". She said she used courage to put God's plan into action. She had also been aided by members of the public in the early minutes of the escape and said that this brought "joy to my heart and helps me understand that although the world is not guaranteed to be safe, there are many good people in it". Riley also described multiple people who had been kind and supportive towards her, even though her family were harsh and blaming in their responses.

Addressing self-blame: Deconstruction questions

- You said that you were "stupid for trusting this man" who assaulted you. Were there things the man who held you captive had said or done that made you trust him?

- Looking back now, with the wisdom you have gained about people who abuse, would you call these things he was saying and doing "tactics"?

- What does it mean to you when you can call these "deliberate tactics"?

- Do you think he used these deliberate tactics on others?

- Given you now know that he has held other people captive[40],
  do you think others were also convinced by these deliberate tactics?

- Does thinking about these things now have any effect on the idea
  that you were "stupid for trusting him"?

Thinking about the other people who had been tricked by this man was in some ways hard for Riley. She said it hurt to think that other people had been through what she went through. However, recalling that other people had been tricked before her destabilised the idea of "being stupid" for trusting him. This was further dismantled as we discussed tactics that various men have used to trick people into entering unsafe situations. These tactics were found in stories from the media, stories from other people Riley knew, and stories from my work with other women. Seeing these more clearly as "deliberate tactics" assisted Riley to consider the amount of planning this man may have put into each time he tricked and captured someone. This located the responsibility with the man who assaulted her, whereas previously the dominant story was that she was responsible for "walking into the situation". This dominant story had been reinforced by her family after they heard what had happened.

Reclaiming life: Meaning-making questions

- You said you spoke to a friend after your escape.[41]
  What was your hope or intention with this?

- What other steps did you take in the time after this ordeal
  to help you get through?

- Despite all that has happened to you, in many ways you have
  still forged the life you wanted. How was this possible?
  What ideas or beliefs did you hold on to in the difficult time
  after the kidnap and escape?

---

[40] Shape the questions to make them relevant to the person. Riley's captor was in the business of sexual slavery and had kidnapped, assaulted and sold other people.

[41] Or joined a support group etc.

- Is there someone in your faith community who supported
  these ideas and beliefs or inspired you in some way?

- Were there particular scriptures, songs or spiritual practices
  that helped you during this time?

- Is there a special meaning or message that these have given you?

- Is there a history of meaningfulness to you of these particular
  scriptures, songs or spiritual practices in your life, or is this
  a newer development/revelation?

- If one of your support team members were here right now and
  I could ask them, what might they be appreciating about the
  way you have forged your life in the direction you wanted?

Riley was able to identify things that she did to keep connected to God
and to community, and particular verses that comforted her. She loved the
metaphor of God being on her team and said that she hadn't previously
thought that God might be affected by her trust and faithfulness. I asked her
whether there were any verses that might challenge the sense of worthlessness,
and Riley was able to think of two. We looked them up on my phone and I
read these out loud while she let them soak over her. Riley decided to read
these again when she got home and to bring them to mind when the voice
of shame or the sense of worthlessness tried to harass her.

At the end of the first session, Riley said that she felt proud of herself
for all the steps she had taken in her life. She said it was a new thought
to consider herself as having acted in partnership with God during the
escape. At the end of the second session, we wondered together whether
this collaboration between her own knowledge and skills, God's wisdom,
and her willingness to listen to God, might help her in the challenges that
anxiety was posing.

After the third session, Riley noted that anxiety was less present in her
daily thoughts. During the next few months, we also looked at "trust" and
how we might know whether someone is trustworthy. We moved from a
binary of trust/no trust to movement (Bird, 2004): that there could be a
building of trust over time, and that there could be some things she might

trust someone with and other areas where she might not trust them. We also talked about her "radar", which alerts her to danger, and the ways she had fine-tuned this radar over time. Riley came up with a plan to ask friends to help her meet their friends. She also joined a new Bible study group and joined a mixed sports club. In these ways she could expand her network and could get to know men slowly. Friends could vet potential boyfriends through knowing them long-term, rather than meeting people through an app. These strategies helped to reduce anxiety about dating.

****

Feedback on similar conversations about religion, spirituality and agency has been that these conversations increase the person's recognition of their own skills, values and agency, enhancing their sense of self-respect and self-worth. There has also been a sense of joy or hopefulness about life when re-membering a connection with God or a faith community, and the ways in which this has been an important support in tough times.

In this chapter I have invited you, the reader, to consider how your own beliefs influence your work, with the hope that self-reflection assists us to address the power we hold in the therapeutic space. I have also shared the ways I have listened out for and actively invited discussion of faith and spirituality in explorations of surviving difficult or traumatic situations. In these explorations, I have kept in mind the intention of supporting people who have felt powerless in their own lives to have an increased sense of agency in not only surviving abuses of power, but also moving towards the hopes they have for their lives.

Reflection

- Which ideas from this chapter might you take up and try?

- What is your guess about the possible effects of taking up and trying out these ideas?

- Which ideas might you leave behind?

- In what ways do you demonstrate respect for the beliefs of others, even if they don't fit with your own beliefs?

- How will you know whether people you meet with are experiencing an increase in sense of agency on account of your conversations or interactions with them?

11.
Weaving the threads into a tapestry

Throughout this book I have been weaving together narrative practices, feminist principles and stories of practice. Coming to the final pages of the book, I invite you, the reader, to step back and look at the tapestry and then move in to focus on particular threads that have caught your attention.

As I revisit these stories, what stands out to me is the remarkable steps that the people I was meeting with were taking in their own lives, despite immense challenges and hardships. These steps may seem small to others, but to do something like attending a playgroup for the sake of their child took much courage for someone who had been repeatedly abused by friends and family. To enter a room of people, let alone build trust with strangers, is immense. I met with many of the women in their homes, and some days we wondered together about what it had taken to even get up, get dressed and open the front door for a conversation with me. I often heard about a desire for life to be even a little bit easier, for some small relief from incredible suffering, and a hope that the lives of their children would be better because of the actions they had taken.

The issues we have explored together have included family and domestic violence, sexual violence, poverty, classism, racism, homophobia and heteronormativity.

Child abuse, sexual violence, and family and domestic violence occur across all social, racial, gender, sexual identity and economic groups. I have met with people from different states of Australia and overseas, from different racial and cultural backgrounds, across various sexualities and genders and from different socioeconomic backgrounds. Stories about being subjected to abuses of power have been common, and the effects on people's lives have been incredibly challenging for them. For some, there was a clear connection between ongoing abuses in childhood and additional hardships such as interrupted education and the use of alcohol and other drugs to alleviate distress. This may have made them more vulnerable to chronic health conditions, poverty and state intervention through child protection services or the "criminal justice" system. Many have experienced this intervention as harmful and violent. These are further injustices.

The free service I worked in was funded for parents, young people and children; however, even though interpersonal violence also occurs in LGBTQIA+ relationships (see Lay, 2017) and against heterosexual men, most of the people I met with were cisgender women in heterosexual relationships. This prompted me to consider patriarchy and the "normalising gaze" (Foucault, 1979; see M. White & Epston, 1990, p. 69). Why are mothers often referred to counselling to address issues related to their children, and fathers rarely so? Why, when there were school meetings, were mothers present and not fathers, even when neither was employed outside the home? Why, when violence was identified within families, was I more comfortable engaging with women than with their male partners?[42] Why was our service mostly used by heterosexual families? Reflecting on questions like these is imperative for accountability about the real impacts of our work, and a continued striving for better practice.

In the context of meeting mainly with cisgender women, I have heard many stories about sexual abuse that had occurred when they were children or in their teens. This had me less focused on men who had been sexually abused as children or teens. Of course, I was aware that abuse of boys and men does occur, and I had heard of the effects on men close to me who had been abused in Catholic and Protestant churches. Occasionally women would speak to me about the effects on their male partner of childhood

---

[42] This has been acknowledged as a phenomenon in many child-protection and family counselling services in which efforts to engage men have, for various reasons, been minimal (Brown et al., 2009). An outcome of this is that women are held accountable for stopping or avoiding the violence used against them and their children, as distinct from those who use violence being held responsible. I join the many practitioners who are trying to remedy these errors in our work.

sexual abuse, but these men did not engage in counselling or other services. I want to acknowledge that while the stories shared in this book were from cisgender women, we do know that many men also have stories to share.[43] Many trans women, trans men and nonbinary folks also have stories of surviving abuse. We need to create honouring spaces for all people to speak about what they have been subjected to and how they have survived. There is much work that still needs to occur to change our culture to address attitudes that condone or perpetuate gendered violence (A. Y. Davis, Dent, Meiners, & Richie, 2022).

Another theme that runs through the stories I have shared is that people always respond to the trauma they are subjected to. Through the writings of Allan Wade (1997), Michael White (2004b, 2005) and Angel Yuen (2007), I have been encouraged to always be on the lookout for responses made by children and young people, even when it is an adult telling their story. I have been excited by the work of Maya Sen (2019) and Shelja Sen (2021) in India, highlighting and celebrating young women's acts of resistance in institutions such as schools and residential care. Evident in the stories I have shared in this book are many actions of survival, of care for others, of resistance or protest, of holding on to precious values. I hope noticing these brings you energy and hope.

Guiding this work has been the feminist principle of seeing the social and political aspects of problems that people encounter in their lives. Connected to this is something I have learnt through social movements: that we are stronger together. In the stories of practice, I have shown how we can connect people to each other and to broader social movements, encouraging voice, solidarity and action. For some people, looking back at history through the lens of feminism has offered a new perspective. We can search for and highlight local knowledge and meaning-making, also known as folk psychology (M. White, 2001), through asking people how their story connects with stories they have heard from friends, social media, podcasts, the arts or traditional media. Using current events and media can be a scaffolding tool to draw out similarities and differences in experiences,

---

[43] For discussion of the myths surrounding men's experiences of sexual violence, and to read about work with Dale, who shared his story with the Royal Commission into Institutional Responses to Child Sexual Abuse, see Donovan (2018) and Donovan & Johns (2022).

and in skills and values utilised in responses to hardship. As narrative practitioners, we are drawing on the work of feminist activists throughout the world who have fought for recognition of the power structures in society that lead to violence, and the intersections of sexism, racism, homophobia, ableism and class-based oppression. These strong women and their allies have agitated for cultural change. A movement that has been particularly influential on the people I work with has been the #MeToo movement, through which women have seen their stories reflected in the stories of others and discovered that they are not alone. This sense of solidarity has spurred people into action. For some, this has taken the form of agitating for change in the public arena. For others, it has meant sharing their story with a friend for the first time.

In addition to sharing people's acts of resistance to violence, in this book I have sought to share stories from the people I have met with in relation to other social issues such as racism, homophobia and heteronormativity. I have sought to describe the learnings I have made over time through the generosity and patience of the people who have let me into their lives.

I have also shared the ways I have listened out for and actively invited discussion of faith and spirituality in explorations of surviving difficult or traumatic situations. In these explorations, I have kept in mind the intention of supporting people who have felt powerless in their own lives to have an increased sense of agency in not only surviving abuses of power, but also moving towards the hopes they have for their lives.

Throughout the book I have invited you, the reader, to consider how your own beliefs, culture and history influence your work. It is my hope that self-reflection can assist us to address the power imbalances that exist in the therapeutic space. I hope that this book invites you to reflect on your own work and experiences of life, to honour your learnings and those who have contributed to those learnings, and to examine areas for further development. I also hope that you will be on the lookout for opportunities to foster connection, solidarity and collective action, large or small. I hope that I have offered practical tools to experiment with, remembering that you are invited to adapt the questions and practices to suit the culture of your local community and the preferences of the people you meet with.

Reflection

- As you have explored the ideas in this book,
  who have you discussed them with?
  Or who might you discuss them with?

- Which ideas or practices might you try out this week?

- Who supports you as you try out new ideas in practice?

References

Australian Bureau of Statistics. (2017). *Personal Safety, Australia: Statistics for family, domestic, sexual violence, physical assault, partner emotional abuse, child abuse, stalking and safety.* https://www.abs.gov.au/statistics/people/crime-and-justice/personal-safety-australia/2016

Australian Human Rights Commission. (2017a). *Bringing them home: Report of the National Inquiry into the Separation of Aboriginal and Torres Strait Islander Children from their Families.* https://humanrights.gov.au/our-work/bringing-them-home-report-1997

Australian Human Rights Commission. (2017b). *Change the Course: National report on sexual assault and sexual harassment at Australian universities (2017).* https://humanrights.gov.au/our-work/sex-discrimination/publications/change-course-national-report-sexual-assault-and-sexual

Australian Human Rights Commission. (2018). *Everyone's business: Fourth national survey on sexual harassment in Australian workplaces (2018).* https://humanrights.gov.au/our-work/sex-discrimination/publications/everyones-business-fourth-national-survey-sexual

Australian Human Rights Commission. (2020). *Respect@Work: National Inquiry into Sexual Harassment in Australian Workplaces.* https://humanrights.gov.au/our-work/sex-discrimination/publications/respectwork-sexual-harassment-national-inquiry-report-2020?mc_cid=1065707e3c&mc_eid=%5bUNIQID%5d – retrieved 07/04/2021.

Australian Institute of Health and Welfare. (2022). *Permanency outcomes for children in out-of-home care: Indicators.* https://www.aihw.gov.au/reports/child-protection/permanency-outcomes-children-indicators/

Australian Institute of Health and Welfare. (2023). *Australia's welfare 2023 data insights* [Catalogue number AUS 246]. Australian Government. https://www.aihw.gov.au/getmedia/d86bae1e-ddc8-45b6-bb85-6e85380d041f/aihw-aus-246.pdf?v=20230829203608&inline=true

Barajas, J., & Bush, D. (2018, September 27). Ford testified. Kavanaugh testified. What did we learn? *PBS News Hour.* https://www.pbs.org/newshour/nation/ford-testified-kavanaugh-testified-what-did-we-learn

Beaudoin, M.-N. (2019). Intensifying the preferred self: Neurobiology, mindfulness and embodiment practices that make a difference. *International Journal of Narrative Therapy and Community Work*, (3), 94–103.

Beckett, S. (2007). Nurturing resistance and refusing to separate gender, culture and religion: Responding to gendered violence in Muslim Australian communities. In A. Yuen & C. White (Eds.), *Conversations about gender, culture, violence and narrative practice: Stories of hope and complexity from women of many cultures* (pp. 43–50). Dulwich Centre Publications.

Bird, J. (2004). *Talk that sings: Therapy in a new linguistic key*. Edge.

Bourdieu, P. (1988). *Homo academicus*. Stanford University Press.

Brown, L., Callahan, M., Strega, S., Walmsley, C., & Dominelli, L. (2009). Manufacturing ghost fathers: The paradox of father presence and absence in child welfare. *Child and Family Social Work, 14*, 25–34.

Bruner, J. (1990). *Acts of meaning*. Harvard University Press.

Burke, T. (2021). *Unbound: My story of liberation and the birth of the Me Too movement*. Flatiron.

Campo, M., & Tayton, S. (2015). *Intimate partner violence in lesbian, gay, bisexual, trans, intersex and queer communities: Key issues*. Australian Institute of Family Studies.

Caulfield, L. (2021). "I am more than the violence I survive": Reflections from the policing family violence storytelling project. *International Journal of Narrative Therapy and Community Work*, (4), 76–93.

Chesler, P. (1972). *Women and madness*. Doubleday.

Chris Dawson, subject of Teacher's Pet podcast, set to be charged with wife's murder. (2019, December 5). *ABC News*. https://www.abc.net.au/news/2018-12-05/chris-dawson-arrested-murder-charges-teachers-pet-podcast/10584024

Contos, C. (2021, March 15). "Do they even know they did this to us?": Why I launched the school sexual assault petition. *Guardian*. https://www.theguardian.com/commentisfree/2021/mar/15/do-they-even-know-they-did-this-to-us-why-i-launched-the-school-sexual-assault-petition

Coumarelos, C., Weeks, N., Bernstein, S., Roberts, N., Honey, N., Minter, K., & Carlisle, E. (2023). *Attitudes matter: The 2021 National Community Attitudes towards Violence against Women Survey (NCAS), Findings for Australia* (Research report, 02/2023). ANROWS.

Crenshaw, K. (1991). Mapping the margins: Intersectionality, identity politics, and violence against women of color. *Stanford Law Review. 43*(6), 1241–1299.

Dalton, A. (2022, December 20). Harvey Weinstein found guilty of rape in Los Angeles trial. *Sydney Morning Herald*. https://www.smh.com.au/world/north-america/harvey-weinstein-found-guilty-of-rape-in-los-angeles-trial-20221220-p5c7p2.html

Dang, M. (2018). Creating ripples: Fostering collective healing from and resistance to sexual violence through friendships. *International Journal of Narrative Therapy and Community Work*, (1), 1–9.

Davis, A. Y., Dent, G., Meiners, E. R., & Richie, B. E. (2022). *Abolition. Feminism. Now*. Haymarket Books.

Davis, V. (2017). My Meeting Place: Rearming ourselves with cultural knowledge, spirituality and community connectedness. *International Journal of Narrative Therapy and Community Work*, (3), 5–16.

Denborough, D. (2008). *Collective narrative practice*. Dulwich Centre Publications.

Denborough, D. (2014). *Retelling the stories of our lives: Everyday narrative therapy to draw inspiration and transform experience*. Norton.

Denborough, D. (2018). *Do you want to hear a story? Adventures in collective narrative practice*. Dulwich Centre Publications.

Denborough, D., & Preventing Prisoner Rape Project. (2005). prisoner rape support package. *International Journal of Narrative Therapy and Community Work*, (2), 29–37.

DiGirolamo, R. (2021, June 1). Adelaide High School students walk out of class to protest against "sexist culture" in their school. *The Advertiser*. https://www.adelaidenow.com.au/education-south-australia/adelaide-high-school-students-walk-out-of-class-to-protest-against-sexist-culture-in-their-school/news-story/b934bd21125b3a605f02b9e5f730fa7e

Donovan, T. (2018). Reclaiming lives from sexual violence. *International Journal of Narrative therapy and Community Work*, (1), 41–48.

Donovan, T., & Johns, D. (2022). *Reclaiming lives from sexual violence: Understanding shame through innovative narrative therapy.* Routledge

Doty, A. (1993). *Making things perfectly queer: Interpreting mass culture.* University of Minnesota Press.

Dowse, K. (2017). Thwarting Shame: Feminist engagement in group work with men recruited into patriarchal dominance. *International Journal of Narrative Therapy and Community Work,* (1), 1–10.

Dulwich Centre Publications. (2004). Narrative therapy and research. *International Journal of Narrative Therapy and Community Work,* (2), 29–36.

Dulwich Centre Publications. (Ed.). (2020). *Yarning with a purpose: First Nations narrative practice.* Dulwich Centre Publications.

Dwyer, C. (Director). (2020). *Brazen hussies* [Documentary film]. Film Camp; Brazen Hussies Film.

Epston, D. (1999). Co-research: The making of an alternative knowledge. In *Narrative therapy and community work: A conference collection* (pp. 137–157) Dulwich Centre Publications.

Epston, D., & White, M. (1992). Consulting your consultants: The documentation of alternative knowledges. In D. Epston & M. White (Eds.), *Experience, contradiction, narrative and imagination: Selected papers of David Epston and Michael White, 1989–1991* (pp. 11–26). Dulwich Centre Publications.

Farrow, R. (2017, October 23). From aggressive overtures to sexual assault: Harvey Weinstein's accusers tell their stories. *The New Yorker.* https://www.newyorker.com/news/news-desk/from-aggressive-overtures-to-sexual-assault-harvey-weinsteins-accusers-tell-their-stories

Faulkner, J. (2020). Responding to women in prison who have used interpersonal violence: A narrative approach to disrupting binaries. In Dulwich Centre (Ed.), *Intersecting stories: Narrative therapy reflections on gender, culture and justice* (pp. 17–42). Dulwich Centre Publications.

Favazza, A. (2011). *Bodies under siege: Self-mutilation, nonsuicidal self-injury, and body modification in culture and psychiatry* (3rd ed.). John Hopkins University Press.

Foucault, M. (1978). The history of sexuality, Vol. 1, An introduction. (R.Hurley, Trans.) Pantheon (Original work published 1976).

Foucault, M. (1979). *Discipline and punish: The birth of the prison.* Peregrine.

Foucault, M. (1980). *Power/knowledge: Selected interviews and other writings.* Pantheon.

Freire, P. (1994). *Pedagogy of hope: Reliving Pedagogy of the oppressed.* Continuum.

Gibson, P. (2013, June 12). We have to stop the creation of another Stolen Generation. *The Guardian.* http://www.theguardian.com/commentisfree/2013/jun/12/stolen-generation-aboriginal-children

Gillard, J. (Ed.). (2022). *Not now, not ever: Ten years on from the misogyny speech.* Penguin.

Grandmothers Against Removals. (2015). *Guiding principles for strengthening the participation of local Aboriginal community in child protection decision making.* https://www.facs.nsw.gov.au/download?file=373233

Handsaker, R. (2012). Opening up the counselling room: The joining of stories as a political act. *International Journal of Narrative Therapy and Community Work,* (3), 1–9.

Hanisch, C. (1969). The personal is political. In In S. Firestone, & A. Koedt (Eds.), *Notes from the Second Year: Women's liberation, major writings of the radical feminists* (pp. 76–78). Radical Feminism.

Hare-Mustin, R. T. (1994). Discourses in the mirrored room: A postmodern analysis of therapy. *Family Process, 33,* 19–35.

Hegarty, T., Smith, G., & Hammersley, M. (2010). Crossing the river: A metaphor for separation, liminality, and reincorporation. *International Journal of Narrative Therapy and Community Work,* (2), 51–58.

Hill, J. (2019). *See what you made me do.* Black Inc.

hooks, b. (1984). *Feminist theory: From margin to center.* South End Press.

hooks, b. (1986). Sisterhood: Political solidarity between women. *Feminist Review, 23,* 125–138. https://doi.org/10.2307/1394725

hooks, b. (1991). Theory as liberatory practice. *Yale Journal of Law and Feminism, 4*(1), 1–12.

hooks, b. (2014). *Feminism is for everybody.* Routledge.

Huggins, J. (2022). *Sister girl: Reflections on tiddaism, identity and reconciliation.* University of Queensland Press.

Hung, S. L. (2011). Collective narrative practice with rape victims in the Chinese society of Hong Kong. *International Journal of Narrative Therapy and Community Work,* (1), 14–31.

Hung, S. L., & Denborough, D. (2013). Unearthing new concepts of justice: Women sexual violence survivors seeking healing and justice. *International Journal of Narrative Therapy and Community Work,* (3), 18–26.

Hush, A. (2020). What's in a hashtag? Mapping the disjunct between Australian campus sexual assault activism and #MeToo. *Australian Feminist Studies, 35*(105), 293–309. https:doi.org/10.1080/08164649.2020.1843997

Jenkins, A. (2009). *Becoming ethical: A parallel, political journey with men who have used abuse.* Russell House.

Kavanaugh hearing: Transcript. (2018, September 27). *Washington Post.* https://www.washingtonpost.com/news/national/wp/2018/09/27/kavanaugh-hearing-transcript/

Kis-Sines, N., Kutuzova, D., Pluznick, R., Russell, S., Denborough, D., Newman, D., White, C., & Anonymous. (2008). Children, parents and mental illness. International Journal of Narrative Therapy and Community Work, (4), 3–14.

Kitzinger, C., & Perkins, R. (1993). *Changing our minds: Lesbian feminism and psychology.* Onlywomen.

Lay, Y. (2017). *Primary prevention of family violence against people from LGBTI communities: An analysis of existing research.* Our Watch. https://www.ourwatch.org.au/resource/primary-prevention-of-family-violence-against-people-from-lgbtiq-communities-an-analysis-of-existing-research/

Lee, P. L., & Pederson, L. (2014, November 10–12). *Responding to multiple, ongoing trauma* [Conference presentation]. 12th International Narrative Therapy and Community Work Conference, Adelaide, Australia.

Leser, D., & Chrysanthos, N. (2021, May 15). Sex, schoolkids and where it all goes wrong. *Sydney Morning Herald.* https://www.smh.com.au/national/sex-schoolkids-and-where-it-all-goes-wrong-20210312-p57a48.html

Lorde, A. (1984). The master's tools will never dismantle the master's house. In A. Lorde (Ed.), *Sister outsider* (pp. 110–113). Crossing Press.

Loveday, H. (2009). From oppression resistance grows. *International Journal of Narrative Therapy and Community Work,* (1). 3–13.

Maisel, R., Epston, D., & Borden, A. (2004). *Biting the hand that starves you: Inspiring resistance to anorexia/bulimia.* Norton.

Massola, J. (2015, June 23). Julia Gillard on the moment that should have killed Tony Abbott's career. *Sydney Morning Herald.* https://www.smh.com.au/politics/federal/julia-gillard-on-the-moment-that-should-have-killed-tony-abbotts-career-20150622-ghug63.html

Maunder, S. (2019, May 19). The Teacher's Pet podcast inspired women to come forward with allegations of sexual abuse by teachers. *ABC News.* https://www.abc.net.au/news/2019-05-15/podcast-inspires-women-to-come-forward-about-school-sexual-abuse/11091426

McPhie, L., & Chaffey, C. (2000). The journey of a lifetime: Group work with young women who have experienced sexual assault. In Dulwich Centre Publications (Ed.), *Extending narrative therapy: A collection of practice-based papers* (pp. 31–60). Dulwich Centre Publications.

Meiners, E. R. (2011). Ending the school-to-prison pipeline/Building abolition futures. *Urban Review, 43,* 547–565. https://doi.org/10.1007/s11256-011-0187-9

Mohanty, C. (2003). *Feminism without borders: Decolonizing theory, practicing solidarity.* Duke University Press.

Moreton-Robinson, A. (2000). *Talkin' up to the white woman: Indigenous women and feminism.* University of Queensland Press.

Morgan, A. (2000). *What is narrative therapy? An easy-to-read introduction.* Dulwich Centre Publications.

Myerhoff, B. (1982). Life history among the elderly: Performance, visibilty, and re-membering. in J. Ruby (Ed.), *A crack in the mirror: Reflexive perspectives in anthropology* (pp. 99–117). University of Pennsylvania Press.

Myerhoff, B. (1986). "Life not death in Venice": Its second life. In V. Turner & E. Bruner (Eds.), *The anthropology of experience* (pp. 261–286). University of Illinois Press.

Newman, D. (2008). Rescuing the said from the saying of it: Living documentation in narrative therapy. *International Journal of Narrative Therapy and Community Work,* (3), 24–34.

Newman, D. (2016). Explorations with the written word in an inpatient mental health unit for young people. *International Journal of Narrative Therapy and Community Work,* (4), 45–57.

NSW Government. (2014). *It stops here: Standing together to end domestic and family violence in NSW.*

Parkes-Hupton, H. (2022, August 30). *Chris Dawson found guilty of murdering ex-wife Lynette in the Teacher's Pet trial: As it happened.* ABC News. https://www.abc.net.au/news/2022-08-30/chris-dawson-verdict-live-blog/101385054

PBS Newshour. (2018, September 28). *"Too often women's memories and credibility have come under assault," Feinstein at Kavanaugh hearing* [Video]. YouTube. https://www.youtube.com/watch?v=7csp9X8iOoI

Pederson, L. (2014, August 4). *Utilising narrative ideas when meeting with people experiencing suicidal thoughts by Loretta Pederson* [Video]. https://dulwichcentre.com.au/utilising-narrative-ideas-when-meeting-with-people-experiencing-suicidal-thoughts-by-loretta-pederson/

Pilkington, E. (2020). Harvey Weinstein convicted of rape at New York trial. *The Guardian.* https://www.theguardian.com/film/2020/feb/24/harvey-weinstein-guilty-trial-charges-verdict

Politicians and judges to be included in Sex Discrimination Act, federal government announces. (2021, April 8). *ABC News.* https://www.abc.net.au/news/2021-04-08/government-responds-sexual-harassment-respect-at-work-report/100055070

Productivity Commission. (2024). *Socio-economic outcome area 12: Aboriginal and Torres Strait Islander children are not overrepresented in the child protection system.* Closing the Gap information repository. https://www.pc.gov.au/closing-the-gap-data/dashboard/se/outcome-area12/out-of-home-care

Reynolds, V. (2013). The problem's not depression it's oppression. In M. Hearn & The Purple Thistle Centre (Eds.), *Stay solid! A radical handbook for youth* (p. 276). AK Press.

Reynolds, V. (2014). Resisting and transforming rape culture: An activist stance for therapeutic work with men who have used violence. *Ending men's violence against women and children,* (Spring), 29–49.

Richardson, C., & Reynolds, V. (2014). Structuring safety in therapeutic work alongside Indigenous survivors of residential schools. *Canadian Journal of Native Studies, 34*(2), 147–164.

Royal Commission into Institutional Responses to Child Sexual Abuse. (2017). *Final Report.* Commonwealth of Australia. https://www.childabuseroyalcommission.gov.au/final-report

Russell, S. (2001). Ethics – A gift from the past. *Dulwich Centre Journal,* (1).

Russell, S. (2006). Gathering stories about growing up with a parent with mental health difficulties. *International Journal of Narrative Therapy and Community Work,* (3), 59–57.

Schechter, S. (1982). *Women and male violence: The visions and struggles of the battered women's movement.* South End Press.

Sen, M. (2019). Working with young people in residential care in India: Uncovering stories of Resistance. *International Journal of Narrative Therapy and Community Work,* (1), 40–50.

Sen, S. (2021). Just Girls: conversations on resistance, social justice and the mental health struggles of women. *International Journal of Narrative Therapy and Community Work,* (1), 60–59.

Sentance, N. (2022, July 12). *Genocide in Australia.* https://australian.museum/learn/first-nations/genocide-in-australia/

Smith, D. (2018, September 28). Kavanaugh hearing puts America's state of disunion in stark relief. *The Guardian.* https://www.theguardian.com/us-news/2018/sep/27/brett-kavanaugh-christine-blasey-ford-hearing-analysis

Stevens, S. (2010). Letter writing: Possibilities and practice. *International Journal of Narrative Therapy and Community Work,* (4), 45–56.

Stout, L. (2010). "Talking about the suicidal thoughts": Towards an alternative framework. *International Journal of Narrative Therapy and Community Work,* (3), 3–15.

Tamasese, T. K. (2007). Preface. In A. Yuen & C. White (Eds.), *Conversations about gender, culture, violence and narrative practice: Stories of hope and complexity from women of many cultures* (pp. v–vii). Dulwich Centre Publications.

Thomas, H. (Host). (2018a). *The Teacher's Pet* [Audio podcast]. The Australian; Crime X.

Thomas, H. (Host). (2018b, 5 July). Hopeless [Audio podcast episode]. In *The Teacher's Pet.* The Australian; Crime X.

Thomas, H. (Host). (2018c, May 23). Cromer High [Audio podcast episode]. In *The Teacher's Pet.* The Australian; Crime X.

Tilsen, J., & Nyland, D. (2010). Resisting normativity: Queer musings on politics, identity and the performance of therapy. *International Journal of Narrative Therapy and Community Work,* (3), 64–70.

Transcript: Donald Trump's taped comments about women. (2016, October 8). *New York Times.* https://www.nytimes.com/2016/10/08/us/donald-trump-tape-transcript.html

Treatment and Rehabilitation Centre for Victims of Torture & Dulwich Centre Foundation International. (2014). *Responding to trauma that is not past: Strengthening stories of survival and resistance.* Dulwich Centre Foundation International.

Turner, V. (1969). *The ritual process: Structure and anti-structure.* Cornell University Press.

Turner, V. (1979). *Process, performance and pilgrimage: A study in comparative symbology.* Concept.

Ussher, J. M., Hawkey, A., Perz, J., Liamputtong, P., Marjadi, B., Schmied, V., Dune, T., Sekar, J. A., Ryan, S., Charter, R., Thepsourinthone, J., Noack-Lundberg, K., & Brook, E. (2020). *Crossing the line: Lived experience of sexual violence among trans women of colour from culturally and linguistically diverse (CALD) backgrounds in Australia.* ANROWS.

van Gennep, A. (1960). *The rites of passage.* University of Chicago Press. (Original work published 1909)

Vygotsky, L. (1986). *Thought and language*. MIT Press.

Wade, A. (1997). Small acts of living: Everyday resistance to violence and other forms of oppression. *Contemporary Family Therapy, 19*(1), 23–39.

Wanganeen, J. (2022). Decolonising child protection discourses using narrative practices. *International Journal of Narrative Therapy and Community Work*, (2), 9–17. https://doi.org/10.4320/OITI8153

Warner, M. (1991). Fear of a queer planet. *Social text, 29*, 3–17.

Warner, M. (1999). *The trouble with normal: Sex, politics, and the ethics of queer life*. Harvard University Press.

White, C. (2016a). Feminist challenge and women's liberation. In C. White (Ed.), *A memory book for the field of narrative practice* (pp. 48–65). Dulwich Centre Publications.

White, C. (2016b). Five radical ideas, splits and things not to leave behind: A conversation with Ron Findlay. In C. White (Ed.), *A memory book for the field of narrative practice* (pp. 19–25). Dulwich Centre Publications.

White, C., & Hales, J. (Eds.). (1997). *The personal is the professional: Therapists reflect on their families, lives and work*. Dulwich Centre Publications.

White, C., & Kamsler, A. (2016). In C. White (Ed.), *A memory book for the field of narrative practice* (pp. 55–56). Dulwich Centre Publications.

White, M. (1992). Deconstruction and therapy. In D. Epston & M. White (Eds.), *Experience, contradiction, narrative and imagination: Selected papers of David Epston and Michael White, 1989–1991* (pp. 109–151). Dulwich Centre Publications.

White, M. (1995a). Naming abuse and breaking from its effects. In M. White (Ed.), *Re-authoring lives: Interviews and essays* (pp. 82–111). Dulwich Centre Publications.

White, M. (1995b). The politics of therapy. In M. White (Ed.), *Re-authoring lives: Interviews and essays* (pp. 82–111). Dulwich Centre Publications.

White, M. (1997). *Narratives of therapists' lives*. Dulwich Centre Publications.

White, M. (2000a). Challenging the culture of consumption: Rites of passage and communities of acknowledgement. In M. White (Ed.), *Reflections on narrative practice: Essays and interviews* (pp. 25–33). Dulwich Centre Publications.

White, M. (2000b). Re-engaging with history: The absent but implicit. In M. White (Ed.), *Reflections on narrative practice: Essays and interviews* (pp. 35–58). Dulwich Centre Publications.

White, M. (2001). Folk psychology and narrative practice. *Dulwich Centre Journal*, (2), 1–37.

White, M. (2004a). *Narrative practice and exotic lives: Resurrecting diversity in everyday life*. Dulwich Centre Publications.

White, M. (2004b). Working with people who are suffering the consequences of multiple trauma: A narrative perspective. *International Journal of Narrative Therapy and Community Work*, (1), 44–75.

White, M. (2005). Children, trauma and subordinate storyline development. *International Journal of Narrative therapy and Community Work*, (3&4), 10–21.

White, M. (2007). *Maps of narrative practice*. Norton.

White, M. (2011). The responsibilities: Working with men who have perpetrated violence. In D. Denborough (Ed.), *Narrative practice: Continuing the conversations* (pp. 98–117). Norton.

White, M., & Epston, D. (1990). *Narrative means to therapeutic ends*. Norton.

Wingard, B. (2015). Carrying the flag and wiping the shame away: An interview with Kerry Major. In B. Wingard, C. Johnson & T. Drahm-Butler (Eds.), *Aboriginal narrative practice* (pp. 8–14). Dulwich Centre Publications.

Wingard, B., Johnson, C., & Drahm-Butler, T. (Eds.). (2015). *Aboriginal narrative practice.* Dulwich Centre Publications.

Wishart, I., & Maeder, R. (2018). Introduction to David Denborough's "Step by step: Developing respectful and effective ways of working with young men to reduce violence". *Journal of Systemic Therapies*, 37(2), 65–66. https://doi.org/10.1521/jsyt.2018.37.2.65

Yuen, A. (2007). Discovering children's responses to trauma: a response based narrative practice. *International Journal of Narrative therapy and Community Work*, (4), 3–18. Dulwich Centre Publications.

Yuen, A., & White, C. (Eds.). (2007). *Conversations about gender, culture, violence and narrative practice: Stories of hope and complexity from women of many cultures.* Dulwich Centre Publications.

www.ingramcontent.com/pod-product-compliance
Lightning Source LLC
Chambersburg PA
CBHW052130270326
41930CB00012B/2831